PITTSFIELD

PITTSFIELD

GEM CITY *in the* GILDED AGE

Carole Owens

Charleston · London

The
History
PRESS

Published by The History Press
Charleston, SC 29403
www.historypress.net

Cover image: The porch at Tor Court looking over the gardens toward the lake. *Photograph by Edwin Hale Lincoln. Courtesy of Gay Kimball Gamage and David Kimball.*

First published 2007

Manufactured in the United Kingdom

ISBN 978.1.59629.408.0

Library of Congress CIP data applied for.

Notice: The information in this book is true and complete to the best of our knowledge. It is offered without guarantee on the part of the author or The History Press. The author and The History Press disclaim all liability in connection with the use of this book.

For my boys—two exceptional men.

And for The Berkshires. A Navaho song says, "There is a way out of every dark mist over the rainbow trail." The Berkshires are my rainbow trail and I continue to honor them.

CONTENTS

PREFACE

The Berkshire Cottages: A Vanishing Era was published in 1984. For the next twenty-two years I studied, taught and wrote about America's Gilded Age. It was a satisfying pursuit; made more so by the fact that the public's interest in and knowledge about the Gilded Age grew during those decades. In 2006, as a Massachusetts Foundation of the Humanities Scholar in Residence, I focused my research on Pittsfield during the Gilded Age—an unexamined part of Berkshire County and Gilded Age history. The result was an exhibition, "Becoming Pittsfield," mounted at the Berkshire Historical Society and a number of newspaper columns in the *Berkshire Eagle*. This book includes some of that material and builds upon it.

ACKNOWLEDGEMENTS

In twenty-five years of research and study there are many people to thank for their knowledge, skill and support. Following are just a few directly related to this book: the board and staff members of the Berkshire Historical Society; Bill Everhart, my editor, the *Berkshire Eagle*; Kathy Reilly and her staff, Berkshire Athenaeum Local History Room; Denis Lesieur, director, Lenox Library; Bob Boland, Tom Blalock and Jack Trowill, Pittsfield residents and historians; Gail Pinna, Dalton history buff; Bill Bartz, historian, Crane & Co.; Kristen Hatt and Kathy Reilly, readers; and Giles Prett, digital imaging specialist, *Fotografix*.

I offer to each of you my deep appreciation and sincere thanks.

The historic photographs are from the collections of:
Chris Baumann
Berkshire Athenaeum
Berkshire Historical Society
Berkshire Scenic Railway Museum
Gay Kimball Gamage and David Kimball
Lenox Library
Alice Rice Allen Olcott
Carole Owens
Gail Pinna
William Russell Allen House Inc.
Williams College Archives and Special Collections

PART I

THE GILDED AGE

INTRODUCING THE GILDED AGE

The Gilded Age was a fifty-two-year period in American history from the close of the Civil War on April 9, 1865, to America's entrance into World War I on April 6, 1917. Since both historic events occurred in April, it was exactly fifty-two years.

It was a time when vast new wealth was disproportionately distributed into a few hands. Deconstructing that sentence provides insight into the era.

The new wealth came from manufacturing. Prior to the Civil War, England, France and Germany led the world in manufactured goods. After the Civil War, America's manufactured goods equaled those of England, France and Germany combined. The young country developed a national transportation system, a national banking system and the concept of a national marketplace. The resulting wealth was vast and the distribution unequal. While a laborer earned $1 a day and a butler in a fine house earned $2 dollars a day, William Henry Vanderbilt earned $10,000 a day. The story of the Gilded Age includes the effect this imbalance had on every level of American society, the American economy and every aspect of American culture.

The nouveau riche wanted nothing less than to create the social stability of a peerage—an American aristocracy. This was no easy task in the context of the Bill of Rights and the Constitution. They displayed their wealth in city palaces and country cottages to visually establish class distinction. Their accomplishments in industry and politics, and their displays in private life, changed the country.

Samuel Clemens named this half century of national sea change the "Gilded Age." The name was generally adopted, and that was the last point of agreement between the writers of the day. Walt Whitman was stimulated; he called the era brawny and optimistic. Twain ridiculed the age as a time of greed, pomposity and "conspicuous ingenuity with just a little soupçon of illegality."[1] Jacob Riis was ashamed. His attempt

The porch at Tor Court looking over the gardens toward the lake. *Photograph by Edwin Hale Lincoln. Courtesy of Gay Kimball Gamage and David Kimball.*

to acquaint the American public with *How the Other Half Lives* (1890) backfired into an anti-immigration movement. Thorstein Veblen condemned "conspicuous consumption" in *The Theory of the Leisure Class* (1899). William Dean Howells was alternately appalled and captivated. He wrote that the elite were dancing on the "crushed and bleeding bodies of the oppressed."[2] Later in a letter, Howells said the great American novel could only be written during the Gilded Age and only about the entrepreneurs. Edith Wharton and Henry James seemed to agree. Wharton wrote, "I should like to assemble and make into a little memorial these fragments [of everyday life during the Gilded Age]."[3] Henry James dedicated himself to "recording the dilemmas of my characters and of these times."[4]

Modern writers also viewed the Gilded Age very differently. Matthew Josephson diminished the age by dividing it into two groups: the "oppressed masses" and the robber barons.[5] In 1976, the Brooklyn Museum of New York called the era the "American Renaissance." Russell Lynes called new millionaires, not robber barons, but tastemakers.[6] The Brooklyn Museum and Russell Lynes viewed the Gilded Age as a cultural coming of age when the elite supported American art forms, imported European art, built museums, libraries and universities and created a new American aesthetic. Eleanor Dwight recognized the Gilded Age as a period that "offers parallels for our time."[7] Ron Chernow compared certain of today's new economic elite with nineteenth century "titans."[8] What we learn from all the authors, past and present, is that the Gilded Age was a complex time not easily distilled into a single verdict.

The story told here is not of villains or heroes, of evil deeds or great ones, but of a time and place and the people who lived then and there. The story of the Gilded Age is certainly about how the wealthy made their money and how they spent it—how enormous wealth was displayed. The Berkshire cottages were "the wings and turrets of outrageous fortune."[9] In their design, size and elaborate decoration, cottages symbolized the age.

The builders called their elaborate, enormous country houses "cottages" for the same reason they called the Atlantic Ocean "the pond"—they loved physical display and verbal understatement. These princes of commerce and barons of industry built city palaces and country cottages to express their economic power and superior social position. The city blocks where they built their palaces, such as Fifth Avenue in New York City, and the country neighborhoods where they built their cottages achieved a mantle of elegance and fame that has lasted for more than one hundred years. The pomp of the late nineteenth century, the grand houses, gowns, jewels and sheer display of the economic elite, galvanized the public's attention then as it does now.

The Gilded Age is also the story of how the other half lived. The city palaces and the country cottages were the only places at that time where you could find rich and poor, black and white, American- and foreign-born living under one roof. A cottage was a reflection of the new socioeconomic order. A Berkshire cottage is a wonderful starting point for telling the story of the Gilded Age—a place where the themes are manifest, and the only place where the man who earned $10,000 a day and the man who earned $1 a day lived together and met daily. Certainly their tasks and stations differed. One paid the bills; the other did the work. One rang the bell for service; the other answered it.

Yet what made the period important? What distinguished this half century, this 20 percent of American history? Simply, it was during the Gilded Age that we became the country we are today—mechanized, motorized, modern and internationally competitive; our government centralized and our citizens viewed as consumers, not just voters. The Jeffersonian ideal of an agrarian society with a gentlemanly and educated electorate—his Arcadia—was replaced with a brawny industrial and manufacturing state. If Thomas Jefferson came back today, it is unclear what he would recognize of modern American government or industry. If J.P. Morgan came back, he would be right at home in understanding corporate America.

Historians and sociologists love to find microcosms—small places that have all the characteristics of a larger society. During the Gilded Age, at least, Pittsfield was such a place. Pittsfield changed its form of government from the pure democracy of the town meeting to a representative democracy with elected

Tor Court, west façade; the sixty-five-room mansion was the most expensive cottage built in Pittsfield. *Photograph by Edwin Hale Lincoln. Courtesy of Gay Kimball Gamage and David Kimball.*

officials. It grew from a small New England town to a city. Its economic base changed from agriculture to industry. It prospered. It welcomed the Gilded Age elite into its midst, and at the same time, created local millionaires by fostering the newest industries:

energy and transportation. The changes in Pittsfield mirrored those in the country. Pittsfield during the Gilded Age was that small place from which all the elements for understanding the era could be extrapolated.

THE COTTAGERS OF PITTSFIELD

They were the gold standard in food, fashion, entertaining and architecture. The cottagers were the dream merchants—their world was filled with clothes, art, equipage, jewelry and houses that few could afford but everyone wanted.

Cottages were seasonal, never primary, residences. One definition of a cottage was "a summer residence with not less than 20 rooms on no fewer than 30 acres."[10] The select towns where cottages were built were known as Gilded Age resorts. They called Newport the "King of Gilded Age Resorts," but that did not preclude Lenox, Bar Harbor and Pittsfield from finding a place on the list of resorts.

At the resorts, cottagers created jobs for builders, groundskeepers, poultry and dairymen, scullery maids, lady's maids, upstairs and downstairs maids, cooks, butlers, footmen, valets, nursery maids, seamstresses and governesses. They created business for the local purveyors of goods. If the new Gilded Age resort was a small New England village such as Lenox, the cottagers changed the economic base, and their coming en masse created a cottage economy.

Reactions of the locals to the coming of the cottagers differed. Some disliked them, as seen in this December 25, 1901 *Berkshire Evening Eagle* "Letter to the Editor":

> *The reign of the summer visitor in Berkshire is already complete enough. These patronizing pleasure seekers fence off our mountains and valleys and forbid the natives to place a foot on their precincts.*

Some merely saw an economic opportunity, as expressed in the 1890 *Sunday Morning Call*:

> *The West part of the city along William and on West Street is where the...summer villas are. City people are coming this way for summer*

homes not just boarding places. It is well known that folks who own property just beyond [the cottagers' places] *can expect good offers.*

And some locals deferred to the cottagers: when a cottager had a garden fête, the judge adjourned court for the day so he and the lawyers could attend.

Many more misunderstood them. A local real estate broker asked for the permission of a cottager before selling an adjoining property to laborers. He assumed the "lord of the manor" would be offended by the possibility.

"Then they work for a living?" the cottager asked.

The real estate agent nodded.

"Good! Sell to them," he replied. "I would rather have activity and industry for my neighbors than some gentleman poor in activity."

The real estate agent was so surprised that he told and retold the story for years.

Many thought cottagers greedy, spending money only for their own pleasure. The cottagers were, for the most part, substantial contributors to their communities, their churches and the arts. It was during the Gilded Age that the concept of eleemosynary giving—individual charitable giving—was initiated and socially supported. In cooperation with the citizens, Pittsfield cottagers built the town's Athenaeum, St. Stephens Episcopal Church and the gate at the town cemetery. Additionally, they placed Tiffany windows in the Congregational Church and helped solve a dispute between railroads that threatened Pittsfield's place as a transportation hub. Other cottagers founded a training school for nurses and supported the purchase of the Colonial Theater from North Adams investors.

Greedy or generous, exclusive and snubbing or social and inclusive, petty or great: Were they any or all of these things? Perhaps their stories will shed light on this question.

THE FIRST COTTAGER

Thomas Allen's contributions to Pittsfield were generous and long lasting. He, along with Pittsfield citizens, built the Athenaeum

and the gates of Pittsfield's cemetery. The Tiffany window in the Congregational Church (placed in honor of his father Jonathan) is called the Allen window. In 1870, as a battle raged between the Housatonic Line (the New York & New Haven Railroad) and the Western Line (the Boston & Albany Railroad) over the train station, Allen stepped in. He used his considerable powers of persuasion to effect a compromise. Had Allen failed, passengers would have detrained at one station and been forced to walk across town to board at another station. Allen succeeded, and the result was the shared train station appropriately called Union Station. The single shared station was a significant contribution to the appeal of the Pittsfield railroad hub.

The story of the first cottager was one of loss, of being cast out and of eventual triumphant return. It was a search for reparation. Thomas Allen was born in Pittsfield but left when his family could no longer feed or shelter him. He ended his days as Pittsfield's first "permanent summer resident"; that is, its first cottager.

Allen's roots ran deep in Pittsfield. The Reverend Thomas Allen arrived in Pittsfield in 1763 as the first Congregational minister. In his letter accepting the post, the reverend wrote in part:

To The People of Pittsfield: Dear Brethren...having sought divine direction, taken the advice of the judicious...I cannot but think it my duty to accept...[and] *to preach among you the unsearchable riches of Christ.*

A good and spiritual man, Allen was also practical enough to consider those "non-unsearchable" riches. His letter concluded:

Not doubting that at your next meeting, you will freely grant forty or fifty cords of wood annually...and some addition to my settlement, either by grant in work, out of generosity, by subscription or whatever way you please...These [words] *from your affectionate friend, Thomas Allen.*[11]

Grandson Thomas Allen seemed to possess the same combination of spiritualism and savvy—goodness and

A fête was hosted by Colonel Richard Lathers at his cottage, Abby Lodge. *Courtesy of the Berkshire Historical Society.*

worldliness—as his grandfather had. Thomas was born in 1813, the fifth son of the ten children of Jonathan Allen. His early childhood was spent in "the ministry lot" on East Street, the home Jonathan had inherited from his father the reverend. Bit by bit the ministry lot was sold to meet contingencies, and finally the house too had to go. Jonathan moved his family to a small, unprepossessing farm a few miles out of town on West Street.

Thomas graduated high school and went to Albany to pursue a degree in law. In 1832, when he was nineteen years old, two things happened. Both were tragic. Cholera broke out in the city of Albany forcing Allen to flee. Upon his return to Pittsfield, he learned that his father had suffered a "large pecuniary loss." Under the circumstances Thomas could not continue his education. Jonathan gave his son twenty-five dollars and said, "I have given you an education. Here are these 25 dollars. That is all I can do for you. Go and take care of yourself."[12]

Glowing biographical sketches of Thomas claimed that he did not resent being cast out of the family circle or leaving Pittsfield. Thomas "went forth with energy and an intention of repaying his father with interest" one sketch said. As future events would prove, however, leaving Pittsfield and the family was a sad loss, and Thomas bent his efforts to achieve a triumphant return and a repayment of sorts.

He traveled countrywide, but every stop brought him more success. He was a law clerk in New York City, earning his law degree through apprenticeship. He was a magazine editor in Washington, D.C., earning many political friends, including one president of the United States. Allen was among those who stood at the foot of President Harrison's bed as he lay dying.

He struck out for Missouri to invest in the western railroad expansion. He was successful and well respected. When his interest turned to politics, Thomas was elected to both the Missouri State Senate and the United States House of Representatives. Thomas married Ann Russell, a young St. Louis woman who possessed both wealth and social position. He was not a man "to be snuffed by a rich marriage." He continued to work in Missouri and Washington, D.C., finally achieving princely wealth with the construction of Iron Mountain Railroad.

Union Station. *Courtesy of the Berkshire Athenaeum.*

In 1854, he finally returned to Pittsfield a successful man of mature years. Immediately, he began to buy back the land that had been the "ministry lot." He had to negotiate a number of sales to piece together the original plot and his original home. He marked the position of his grandfather's house, the rectory, with a stand of locust trees. To one side, he built his cottage, Eagle's Nest.

Thomas endeavored to hire the best to design an Allen house on the Allen plot that testified to Allen solvency and success. He selected the architect J.W. Priest. It is said that Thomas gave only one instruction to his architect: "I must have large bedrooms."

Priest distinguished himself as an ecclesiologist—one versed in the science of church architecture and decoration. Eagle's Nest was the last building he designed. He was able to complete the cottage, but died the following year. Priest was a founding member of the American Institute of Architecture and was recalled at the meeting held August 2, 1859. Two of the greatest architects of the day spoke. President Richard Upjohn called Priest one of its most valuable members and "the best of men." Calvert Vaux read the following resolution:

Resolved: That the Institute hereby expresses and desires to put upon record its sincere regret at the loss of one, who professionally and personally was highly esteemed by his brethren of this body.

When complete, Eagle's Nest was an architectural gem. Eagle's Nest was built of indigenous Berkshire limestone, as were the stables behind. The symmetrical building had Gothic detail and was grand in size. There were large, airy bedrooms that looked down upon the manicured lawns and gardens.

The ground floor had a formal dining room, living room and library. The interior appointments reflected the family's world travels and good taste, including a large Limoges vase, Japanese bronzes and Florentine tapestries.

Although the façade was symmetrical, the front and rear elevations were not. To capture a clear, unobstructed view of Mount Greylock, approximately twelve miles away, the rear of the house was four stories while the front was only three stories. The front windows afforded a view of the Pittsfield town center.

The Athenaeum. Athenaeum is the Greek name for an institution that promotes learning. The Pittsfield Athenaeum was not only a library but also a museum. *Courtesy of the Berkshire Athenaeum.*

The house was finished in 1858; ready for Thomas to take triumphant possession, repairing his father's losses.

Allen was not finished. He purchased the old farm on West Street that his father had lost. He added land on both sides and established Taconic Lodge. The son had returned and reclaimed the Allen properties. Thomas turned his energy and resources to improving his beloved Pittsfield, and he was beloved in return to the end of his days. Over the door of the Athenaeum, carved in stone, are the words: "This tribute to science, art, and literature is the gift of Thomas Allen to his native town."

THE PATRICIAN

In 1869, Colonel Richard Lathers purchased nine farms and combined them to create his estate named for his wife, Abby. Lathers, of South Carolina, New York and Pittsfield, invested in commerce, agriculture, insurance, banking and railroads. In turn, these investments richly rewarded him. His art collection of old masters, "collected to educate my family," was renowned. He was even better known as a man of substance who lived among his neighbors "in perfect mutual respect and harmony."

The Lathers family on the porch of Abby Lodge. *Courtesy of the Berkshire Historical Society.*

Eagle's Nest, built on the site of the first Allen residence in Pittsfield. *Courtesy of the Berkshire Athenaeum.*

A millionaire twice over, he was treated as a patrician. Lathers married Abby Thurston, a relative of Thomas Melville, Herman Melville's uncle. In 1882, his son, Richard Jr., married Miss Anne Morewood, a cousin of Herman Melville, thereby connecting the Lathers family to the family of Herman Melville twice in two successive generations.

Lathers was able to continue in business successfully throughout the Civil War. This was singular because he was born and raised in South Carolina and before, during and after the Civil War, he was able to conduct business in New York City.

The secret to Lathers's ability to conduct business with anyone, anywhere, was charm and a sense of humor. In the

Gilded Age, a family crest had more social worth than a Cartier necklace because nouveau riche could amass great wealth but not grand ancestors. Many lied about their lineage; none joked about it. That is, except Lathers. In 1869, as a retired gentleman of means, he was asked about his forefathers. He replied, "I know some men claim four fathers; I had but one." In fact, he rose to financial heights from simple beginnings as a Scotch-Irish immigrant. He never hid the fact; instead he publicly pronounced that he made his way by using his "Scotch caution, toning down [his] Irish impulsiveness, and seeking a land, as all Irish do, that insures their equality and protects their rights."

THE SON AND HEIR

Like his father before him, William Russell Allen built two estates in Pittsfield. His Queen Anne cottage on East Street close to the town center reportedly had one hundred rooms. It did not in actuality have one hundred rooms, but in an age when one thousand square feet was considered an acceptable size for a family home, the thirteen-thousand-square-foot William Russell Allen House may have appeared to have that many.

The house, completed in 1885, was exceptional in its selection of building materials. For example, at a distance the exterior cladding appeared to be cedar shingles but was actually made of hand-wrought terra cotta tiles. The interior entrance hall was laid with eight hundred pounds of Missouri granite. The formality and beauty of the interior appointments was rarely surpassed even in a "gilded" age.

The cottage was surrounded by beautiful gardens originally tended by Frederick S. Fowler. However, Fowler left William Russell Allen's employ in 1893 to become head gardener at Shadow Brook, the cottage of Anson Phelps Stokes. There is no indication why he left—perhaps it was because Shadow Brook actually did have one hundred rooms, or perhaps it was because Shadow Brook, not located in town, had hundreds more acres. Whatever the reason for leaving Pittsfield, when he left Shadow Brook in 1895, the reason was crystal clear. For two

years, Fowler had incurred debts in his employer's name and then appropriated the checks and cash given to him by Stokes to settle the debts. Foul indeed, and it got fouler: there was no trace of Fowler; he skipped town, and when he did, he left his wife and children behind. The amount in question was $7,000 (almost $100,000 in 2007 dollars). Fowler was never found; nor were the funds.

There were also scandals—scandals of a different sort—upstairs. Alice Maud Allen (called Maud) was the sister of William Russell, great-granddaughter of the reverend and youngest daughter of Thomas.

On the evening of June 20, 1888, Charles Atwater married Alice Maud Allen. Charles was also the great-grandson of a minister at Westfield. He came to Pittsfield as a clerk and bookkeeper in the Pomeroy store on West Housatonic and worked his way up and into the best business circles of the city.

The *Berkshire Evening Eagle* reported that it was the social event of the season. The *Pittsfield Sun* said it was "the most brilliant society event seen in this county in years." The ceremony was scheduled for 8:00 p.m. at the First Church in Pittsfield, but guests and curious onlookers began gathering outside at 7:15 p.m. The roads were thick with carriages and the grassy areas clogged with the curious.

Upon entering the church, those lucky enough to have an invitation found an exceptional sight. It was "festooned and wreathed" in every corner with vines, laurel, palms and hundreds of roses. The roof of the church was strung with electric lights—tiny spots twinkling like stars in the vaulted darkness.

It was a unique and astonishingly beautiful wedding. The bride did not wear white. Maud Allen wore a gown of gold cloth with an "old" lace veil. Diamonds cascaded down the dress front and shone in the bride's ears and at her neck. She did not carry flowers. It was the bridesmaids who wore white silk gowns and carried bouquets of pink roses. The groom did not wait at the altar for his bride. At the same time that the bride walked down the center aisle, escorted by her brother William Russell Allen, the groom walked down the east aisle. They met at the altar where young members of the very best families surrounded the bride and groom.

William Russell Allen House. *Courtesy of William Russell Allen House Inc.*

In the bride's party were young ladies from the Allen, Campbell and Atwater families. Standing up for the groom were gentlemen from the Colt, Pomeroy, Tucker and Dwight families.

After the ceremony, Mr. and Mrs. Charles Atwater entertained their many guests at Eagle's Nest on East Street. All day long carts and carriages ferried back and forth from the train station, delivering food, flowers and an orchestra from New York City. Delmonico's served a sumptuous dinner, and at the stroke of midnight, the bride and groom were whisked away. They boarded a train for New York and then a ship of the Cunard Line for a three-month honeymoon in Europe. It was a fairytale beginning for an obviously blessed couple.

The excitement generated was typical of a Gilded Age society wedding, but this wedding also united prominent Berkshire families from Pittsfield and South County. An Atwater-Allen wedding drew into the larger family circle many of the best and most illustrious families of the day: the Allens, the Beechers, the Marquands and, when Charles's sister Lucy married Matthew Dickinson Field, the Fields. It was a great day in The Berkshires.

With such exceptional lineage—the financial acumen of the Allens, the talent of Harriet Beecher Stowe and Henry Ward

Beecher, the sophistication of the Marquands and the brains and accomplishments of, for example, Supreme Court Justice Stephen Field—their children also thrived. Charles and Maud's son, Russell Atwater, became a prominent engineer. Lucy and Matthew's daughter, Rachel Field, became a well-known author. However, Charles and Maud's golden life came to an abrupt end when Charles was forty-four years old.

They were visiting London when Charles was stricken with typhoid fever. He was confined to bed in a hotel, but in delirium, he wandered out and disappeared. A fellow hotel guest, Louis Lombard, led a search party. Charles was found and returned to bed, but died soon after. In her grief Maud turned to Lombard, and the family sensed trouble.

At the William Russell Allen House in Pittsfield, the family gathered with the serious purpose of discouraging Maud from marrying Lombard—it was not that Lombard had no money; it was that he was not of their circle. However, Maud did marry Lombard. If in an age of gleeful gossip columns silence meant peace, then their marriage was successful.

Today, the William Russell Allen House—the last of the Allen houses left in Pittsfield and the last vestige of the Allen contribution to the growth of Pittsfield—stands vacant and in need of restoration.

The 1,250-acre Allen Horse Stock Farm was established in 1886 and boasted a private racecourse and a 100- by 250-foot horse barn. William Russell was a racehorse man at a time when the southern United States held the monopoly on horse breeding. He was an officer in the National Trotting Association and president of the American Association of Horse Breeders.

William Russell believed that racehorses could be bred in a cold climate, and he set about to prove it. He silenced all doubters and proved that racehorses could in fact be bred in a cold climate when, in 1892, his horse, King Kremlin, bred on the Allen farm in Pittsfield, set the world's racing speed record by running the one mile in 2.07 minutes and was proclaimed to be "the fastest horse now alive." In a 1902 article, the Allen farm experiment was reported successful: "There is no question that

Allen farm private racecourse and barn. *Courtesy of William Russell Allen House Inc.*

next to the famous Blue Grass country of Kentucky, Berkshire County stands second and perhaps fully equal."[13]

By 1912 William Russell sold a descendent of Kremlin's to the czar of Russia, and the following year, the Allen farm set more records and won more purse money than any other horse farm in the country.

Another thoroughbred lived at Allen farm: the caretaker was famed photographer Edwin Hale Lincoln.

THE CHICAGO COLONY

New York considered itself at the center of the Gilded Age social world. There were those who believed there were other social centers worthy of note, but New York scoffed—New York society was *the* society. It was a blow to such certainty when Chicago won the competition and became the site of the World's Columbian Exhibition in 1893 (also called the Chicago World's Fair). Still, New York elite populated the best resorts, and most Berkshire cottagers had their primary residence in New York City. Most, but not all: the majority of Pittsfield cottagers came from Chicago.

William Russell Allen farm. *Courtesy of William Russell Allen House Inc.*

Allen Horse Stock Farm, main gate. *Courtesy of William Russell Allen House Inc.*

It may have been Mrs. O'Leary and her cow that started a fire that devastated many, but it created an unprecedented opportunity for a few. After the Great Chicago Fire of 1871, the city was rebuilt, and Chicago fortunes were made, not for the first time.

George H. Laflin was born in Pittsfield, lived in Connecticut and made his fortune in Chicago real estate after 1871. The city Laflin and many others rebuilt was a bigger and better Chicago. Laflin also invested in the Dalton papermaking business, Crane & Co. He was a cousin of Mrs. Zenas Marshall Crane and also related by his marriage to Mary Brewster. Between paper and real estate, Laflin was a very wealthy man. He bought land on East Housatonic for his summer residence. The cottage remained in the family after his death when it became the summer cottage of his only daughter, Chicago socialite Mrs. Elija Whitehead.

"Money answereth all things,"[14] or does it? Henry W. Bishop Jr. was born in Lenox, the son of Judge Bishop. After finishing law school, he went west to Chicago and established himself. Bishop returned to The Berkshires a man of substantial means and built his summer cottage, Wiaka, in Pittsfield.

In August 1884 his wife, Jessie Pomeroy Bishop, died; in September his son, Henry W. Bishop III, contracted peritonitis. Henry III suffered for eleven months as the disease "baffled medical skill." In October 1885 the afflicted father stood and spoke at his son's funeral. "My son left me just as he was

Edwin Hale Lincoln. *Courtesy of the Lenox Library.*

The Lincoln children (Leo, Almon, Norman, Emma and Bernard) and their mother, Hattie, play ball beside the caretaker's house at Allen farm. *Photograph by Edwin Hale Lincoln. Courtesy of the Berkshire Athenaeum and Daryl Lincoln Marty.*

Wiaka. *Courtesy of Berkshire Athenaeum.*

entering into manhood before he could make a mark for himself. Naturally I want him to be remembered." Following the tradition of Pittsfield cottagers, he made a significant contribution to the town. "During his lingering illness I came to know the inestimable value of trained scientific nursing." As a memorial to his son, Bishop funded the Henry W. Bishop III Memorial Training School for Nurses.

In 1889 Elijah Pope Sampson bought the Daniel Sprague property on William Street and spent $100,000 building his "new colonial mansion." It was such a startling amount to spend on a single dwelling that it was considered newsworthy and reported in all the local papers.

Sampson made his fortune in the oilcloth manufacturing business. His factory in New Jersey was the largest in the country. When he died in 1893, his wife and son, Alden Sampson, decided to make the William Street cottage their permanent home.

In 1902 Alden married Lena Wyman. The couple remained in Pittsfield, and Alden assembled the first automobiles ever made in Berkshire County. In the June 1902 edition of *Lenox Life*, a local society paper, Mrs. Alden Sampson was called "the foremost woman automobilist."

The article then stated: "It remains an inexhaustible subject whether women may be trusted to drive automobiles." As the article went on, however, it was clear that it was written by a very liberal reporter who concluded, "Some time it will become self-evident that women are better fit to drive automobiles [than men]." The reason was that only the best of women—the bravest, smartest and most physically agile—would attempt the feat, while any and all men, of varying abilities, were anxious to get behind the wheel.

The article was an interesting insight into early reactions to the automobile. In Chicago, it was further reported, automobilists were required to take licensing examinations. An exam had two parts: the medical, to determine if one had a weak heart or was colorblind, and the operation test. The check for a weak heart was necessary as cars stopped and accelerated abruptly. The operation exam was taken in a specific type of vehicle, and the license was issued for that type only: gasoline, steam or electric. It is interesting that we began our affair with automobiles with a choice of propulsion.

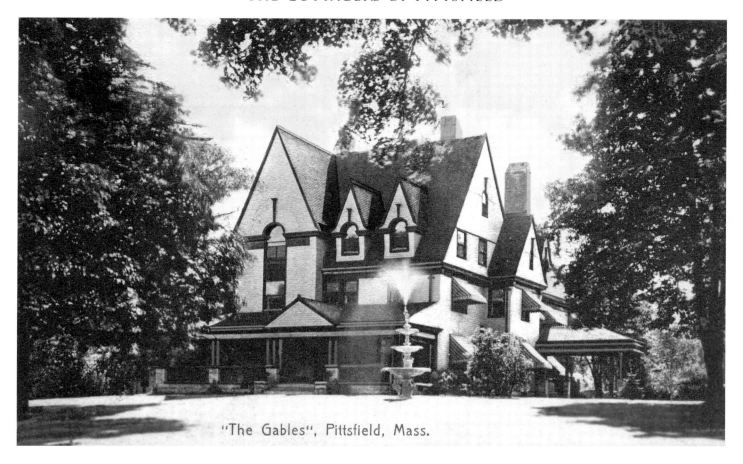

"The Gables", Pittsfield, Mass.

The Gables. *Courtesy of the Berkshire Athenaeum.*

In 1905, Alden opened one of the first truck manufacturing companies in Pittsfield, the Sampson Truck Manufacturing business on the site of the old L. Pomeroy's Sons mill. Early Sampson Truck catalogues and photographs indicate that Alden made as much money by using his trucks to haul Pittsfield goods as by selling them. He operated the business until his premature death in 1909. In 1911 his wife sold the company to the United States Motor Company, but the United States Motor Company ceased operations the following year, and the Sampson truck disappeared from the streets of Pittsfield.

Wirt Dexter Walker, a Chicago lawyer, had a robust bank account and a poor constitution. He believed in the healing powers of mountain air. At twelve hundred feet above sea level, with mountains rising up to eight hundred feet above that, Walker believed Pittsfield could heal him.

In 1888 he purchased land on West Street. For two years, it was anticipated that he would build a new cottage matching the $100,000 spent by fellow Chicagoan and Pittsfield cottager, Elijah Pope Sampson. Finally, in 1890, Walker hired Pittsfield architect H. Neil Wilson to build his cottage.

Cottage of E.P. Sampson. *Courtesy of the Berkshire Athenaeum.*

Pittsfield Sun, June 8, 1890: The return of Wirt D. Walker from his European trip...revives the report that he will carry out his long cherished plan of an elegant summer residence or villa on the West shore of Lake Onota. Architect H. Neil Wilson has submitted plans.

H. Neil Wilson was a Pittsfield architect. It was unusual to hire local architects. Most cottagers sought professionals in New York or Boston. Walker must have had an eye for talent, though, because three years later, in 1893, Wilson completed Shadow Brook, the cottage of Anson Phelps Stokes, and the largest private residence ever built in America to that date.

Blythewood was a 450-acre estate with 250 acres cultivated. In addition to the main house, Wilson designed and oversaw the construction of the outbuildings, including laundry facilities, servants' quarters, superintendent's residence, two barns, two farmhouses, dairy, coach house, wood house, icehouse, gatehouse, greenhouse and gardener's residence.

Wilson designed a cottage with twelve bedrooms and seven baths, electric lights and an internal telephone system. It is interesting to note that while many cottagers favored neoclassic, Elizabethan or Tudor designs, these Chicago cottagers often asked for modern architecture. Over one hundred years old, Blythewood still looks contemporary.

Blythewood Farms. *Courtesy of Berkshire Athenaeum.*

His cottage complete, Walker assured his many friends that his health was improving. Unfortunately, he was wrong. A sudden unexplained fever in late 1896 rendered him blind, and in April 1899 he died. Walker was thirty-nine.

Walker's death was reported with due solemnity and respect in newspapers all over the country. However, when the contents of his will were discovered, there were screaming headlines above the fold: "Will forbids widow to remarry!" "Must live alone or forfeit inheritance!" "Widow disinherited if she remarries!" "Walker controls from the grave!" Drama was high and speculation a rich mix. What had the young widow, Marie Winston Walker, done to earn such a punishment? Alternatively, did Walker show signs of mania before his death? Was his wife a prisoner to his insane jealousy? The widow did not speak but receded into a dignified mourning. For two years there was silence. Her proper behavior earned her widespread sympathy. Then, the tidal wave hit.

Mrs. Walker announced her engagement and the press went wild. The headlines were even bigger when it was discovered that the man was relatively poor. The American public wanted to know: Would the widow choose love or money? It was truly a delicious story. The will clearly contained the words "as long as she remains my widow." Would anyone give up a fortune for love? Finally something had to be done to stem the tide of ink. Mrs. Walker spoke out. The will left her a wealthy woman unconditionally. There was but one exception: Blythewood. Walker's will read, in part, that his wife Marie Winston Walker could retain Blythewood only "as long as she remains my widow." If she remarried, Blythewood became the property of the Wirt D. Walker Art Gallery in Chicago. Mrs. Walker relinquished Blythewood without protest and walked down the aisle into the arms of the man she loved.

Trustees of the Walker Art Gallery sold Blythewood to John Alden Spoor in 1905. When he died in 1926, Spoor was chairman of the board of the Union Stockyards and Transit Company in Chicago, and his estate was valued at $1.4 million ($15.5 million in 2007 dollars). Born in New York, Spoor arrived in Chicago in 1886 to take up a position as manager of the Wagner Palace Car Company. He followed a tried and true Chicago prescription: make money in railroads and invest it in banks. Spoor was a prominent financier and generous contributor to hospitals, libraries and historical societies. He sold Blythewood to a group of Pittsfield investors two years before his death.

After Thomas Allen's death, his heirs sold Taconic Lodge to Henry C. Valentine, a varnish-manufacturing tycoon. Valentine enlarged the property significantly by purchasing Elmwood, the neighboring estate of the Honorable Edward Learned. Valentine cultivated a large part of the estate, and renamed it Taconic Farm.

Taconic Lodge, built by Thomas Allen and sold to a Chicago millionaire. *Courtesy of Berkshire Athenaeum.*

The gatehouse of Taconic Farm. *Courtesy of Berkshire Athenaeum.*

In the summer of 1907, Valentine rented Taconic Farm to Colonel and Mrs. Prentice of Chicago. Mrs. Prentice was the former Alta Rockefeller, daughter of John D. Rockefeller. Colonel Parmelee Prentice was a Chicago attorney who dreamed of becoming an experimental farmer. The Prentices were in Berkshire County searching for land to establish their model farm. They thought they found the perfect location when they saw Taconic Farm. They rented it in anticipation of purchasing; however, it was not to be.

That same summer President Theodore Roosevelt, the "Trust Buster," decided it was time to take on Standard Oil. A subpoena was issued for its owner, John D. Rockefeller. The subpoena would have been sufficient to fuel a dozen newspaper articles, but when Rockefeller ducked the subpoena and vanished, it was international news. Speculation was rife. Where could the richest man in the world hide? The answer was: anywhere he pleased. Every corner of the planet received some attention as a potential hideout for the richest man in the world. Everywhere except Pittsfield.

On June 29, 1907, George Stokes was a newsboy on the New York-New Haven line. As he passed from car to car selling his papers, he saw the old man with the scrawny neck and the ill-fitting suit. George did not disturb him; he didn't look like a fellow with the price of a newspaper. Stokes passed the conductor on his rounds collecting tickets. The conductor had the same reaction—the old man didn't look like anyone who could afford a Pullman ticket. As the train pulled into Union Station at Pittsfield at 8:30 p.m., both men were confused as they watched the "poor old man" get helped down from the train by a liveried chauffeur and escorted to a black limousine. Who was this guy?

The conductor left the station and hurried to tell his cousin the story. The cousin worked at the Pittsfield Post Office and thought he'd seen that fancy black car. The newsboy walked up to the Wendell Hotel and found Alfred C. Daniels, a reporter for the *Pittsfield Journal*. He told his tale. Both conductor and newspaper boy were telling a tale about the strangeness of life—how you can't judge a book by its cover and how you just never know—but the reporter wondered, "Could it be?" If only Daniels had known that a few hours earlier, the telegraph man at Pittsfield received the message "He is coming tonight," but the telegraph man told no one of the strange communiqué.

The next morning, *Journal* reporter Walter E. Lewis looked out the window and saw Colonel Prentice outside Backman's Livery Stable, opposite his office on North Street. He heard the tale of the old man on the train from his colleague Daniels. Lewis stepped across and asked Prentice if, by chance, his father-in-law, John D. Rockefeller, was staying at Taconic Farm. Prentice's answer was quite a surprise: "I will give anyone who can prove that $50,000."

With that non-denial denial, Lewis decided it must be true—as the world was scoured, Rockefeller slipped away to his daughter and son-in-law's place in Pittsfield. To print the story, Lewis had to confirm it. The hunt was on. Reporters spilled into Pittsfield. Exits to the farm were blocked. Approaches to the main house were rebuffed. The siege of Taconic Farm went on. Finally Mr. Rockefeller came forth.

"Are you Mr. Rockefeller?" the local policeman asked.

"I am," said the thin man standing at the front door in a bathrobe; and at that, the richest man in the world accepted the president of the United States' subpoena from a local Berkshire policeman on the steps of a Pittsfield farmhouse.

Rockefeller seemed calm and resigned, but Alta Rockefeller Prentice was distraught. She refused to remain at Taconic Farm. Any purchase of the rental property was declared to be impossible. That is why the Prentice model farm, Mount Hope, ended up in Williamstown instead of Pittsfield.

In 1908, less than a year after Rockefeller was served on the steps of Taconic Farm, 160 acres of the three-hundred-plus-acre Taconic Farm were sold by Valentine to Warren and Evaline Kimball Salisbury. Mr. Salisbury was a manufacturer of rubber goods in Chicago. Mrs. Salisbury's family founded the Kimball Piano and Organ Company—one of the largest manufacturers of pianos and organs during the Gilded Age. More to the point, the Prentices were close friends. As Colonel and Mrs. Prentice continued their search of Berkshire County for land for their model farm without bad memories attached, they recommended Taconic Farm to the Salisburys. The Salisburys liked the farm as much as the Prentices had, and they were friends with other Pittsfield cottagers from Chicago: Henry Bishop, Dr. Frederick Coolidge and John Alden Spoor. They bought the property.

They hired the New York architectural firm of Walker and Gillette to tear down the old house and design their cottage.

Colonel Parmelee and Alta Rockefeller Prentice in a chauffeur-driven automobile. *Courtesy of Williams College Archives and Special Collections.*

Aerial photo of Mount Hope. *Courtesy of Williams College Archives and Special Collections.*

Tor Court, front façade. *Photographer Edwin Hale Lincoln. Courtesy of Gay Kimball Gamage and David Kimball.*

Alexander Stewart Walker and Leon Narcisse Gillette formed a successful architectural firm in the early part of the twentieth century. The firm was known for its sophisticated designs and was responsible for the French Consulate on Fifth Avenue in New York as well as a dozen Long Island and Tuxedo Park estates.

The Salisburys spent $800,000 building their country house. George William Sheldon, in *Artistic Country-Seats*, reported that only two of one hundred country houses built during that period cost over $200,000—even twenty years later, $800,000 was a prodigious sum.[15] When they were done, Mr. and Mrs. Salisbury had a sixty-seven-room cottage of stone and stucco with Tuscan columns. The formal dining room was thirty square feet, and the grand salon was twenty-five by fifty feet. It was, without doubt, one of the most beautiful and most expensive of all the Berkshire cottages. They named it Tor Court.

Tor (High Hill) Court was aptly named, set as it was on a hill above the lake. Berkshire cottages were modeled after European county seats. They were self-sustaining, and Tor Court had a farm with chickens, horses and a dairy, as well as a greenhouse and apple and pear orchards. The gardens included a formal

Tor Court Farm. *Photograph by Edwin Hale Lincoln. Courtesy of Gay Kimball Gamage and David Kimball.*

rose garden, cutting garden, a grape arbor and berry patch, in addition to uncultivated woods and fields. A private boathouse was built on the lakeshore.

The number of people needed to maintain Tor Court, or any of the Berkshire cottages, varied but was never fewer than eight indoors and twenty outdoors under the direction of a single superintendent of grounds or a number of superintendents assigned to the farm, the animals, the greenhouses and the formal gardens.

Tor Court still stands today and is now Hillcrest Hospital.

Dr. Frederick Coolidge of Boston married Elizabeth Penn Sprague of Chicago in November 1891. In 1904, they hired the Pittsfield architectural firm of Harding and Seaver to

design their first Pittsfield cottage, Upwey Field, on West Street. Like Wirt Walker, Dr. Coolidge believed that the high altitude and dry weather of Pittsfield were restorative. When his health began to fail, the family spent more and more time in Pittsfield. After her husband's death in 1915, Elizabeth Coolidge gave Upwey Field to the Berkshire School for Crippled Children in his memory. She built her second Pittsfield cottage on South Street. A musician, Elizabeth called the cottage her "Temple of Music," and there she founded the Berkshire Chamber Music Festival at South Mountain.

In May 1934, Henry Hadley saw the horse ring and rolling green lawn of Bonnie Brier, the Dan Hanna estate in

THE COTTAGERS OF PITTSFIELD

Tor Court salon. *Photograph by Edwin Hale Lincoln. Courtesy of Gay Kimball Gamage and David Kimball.*

Upwey Field. *Courtesy of Berkshire Historical Society.*

Stockbridge. He exclaimed that it would be a perfect orchestra circle for music "under the stars."[16]

Virtually forgotten today, Hadley was a small, dapper man with polished manners. He was a composer and conductor associated with the New York Philharmonic Orchestra, and father of the idea that became the Tanglewood Music festival. He brought his idea to Gertrude Robinson Smith of Stockbridge. Before committing to Hadley's plan, Robinson Smith consulted four friends: Miss Mabel Choate of Naumkeag, Mrs. Carlos de Heredia of Wheatleigh, Mrs. Bruce Crane of Dalton and Mrs. Elizabeth Sprague Coolidge of Pittsfield.

Coolidge's opinion was of particular importance to Robinson Smith. Her experience with the South Mountain concerts was invaluable, and Robinson Smith anticipated that Coolidge would be a major financial supporter.

In the initial stage, Coolidge was enthusiastic. She proclaimed The Berkshires the ideal spot for symphonic music under the stars, and the Berkshire Symphonic Festival was born. The first concerts were planned for August 1934 at the Dan Hanna farm. The South Mountain concerts were on Friday night, Saturday night and Sunday afternoon. Out of consideration for Coolidge, the first Berkshire Symphonic Festival concerts were planned on Thursday night, Saturday afternoon and Sunday night.

By 1936 the New York Philharmonic and Hadley were gone, and the Boston Symphony (BSO) had arrived. In 1937 the Tappan family gave their 210-acre estate, Tanglewood, to the BSO. Tanglewood Music Festival continued to grow in popularity, the schedule expanded and finally there were concerts on Friday night, Saturday night and Sunday afternoon in direct conflict with South Mountain. Mrs. Coolidge was not pleased. She wrote:

> *The Tanglewood music interferes with us* [the South Mountain Concert schedule]. *Please let me know if you have any definite suggestions about the rescue of South Mountain and the Temple of Music.*

Tanglewood found no solution, if indeed they looked for one, so in 1942, Coolidge withdrew her support. She gave $60,000 (about $624,000 today) to build Coolidge Auditorium for Chamber Music in the Library of Congress, Washington, D.C.,

Bald Head Farm. *Courtesy of the Boston Symphony Orchestra.*

instead of Tanglewood. Notwithstanding her ultimate desertion, her early support was crucial in creating a music festival in The Berkshires.

Clifford Buckingham, a Chicago millionaire, made his money by building grain elevators and investing the profits in establishing Chicago banks.

In 1877, he built a cottage on West Street in Pittsfield next door to Thomas Allen's Taconic Lodge, and just east of where Wirt Walker would build Blythewood. In fact it was at the Buckingham cottage that Walker stayed while Blythewood was being built.

Buckingham continued to summer in Pittsfield with his children, Clarence and Kate, until his death in 1912. Two years later, daughter Kate abandoned the Pittsfield colony where she had summered for most of her life and, according to the local newspaper, she became "the first of the Chicago Colony to move to Lenox."

A string of tragedies beginning in 1899 may have caused Kate to leave Pittsfield after so many years. In 1899, the spectacular fifty-five-room Buckingham cottage in Pittsfield burned to the ground. In 1900, her friend, H.B. Daniels, died in Pittsfield at just thirty-four years of age. Kate never married. One year after her father died, her brother Clarence died while still a relatively young man. The deaths left Miss Kate Sturges Buckingham one of the wealthiest women in America and perhaps one of the saddest. Her memories of Pittsfield were of death and destruction—she sought property in Lenox.

When Kate purchased the Lenox land, neighbors feared she would build "Buckingham Palace." Far from a palace, Bald Head Farm was distinctly modest for the times and for a woman of her wealth. It boasted, however, one of the most spectacular views in the Berkshire Hills. In her understated cottage, Kate lived a quiet life.

She did not, as did others in her financial position, throw lavish parties or, according to the society columns, attend them. She ordered that her name be removed from the *Social Register*. Instead she became a philanthropist, but if anyone ever tried to thank her for her generosity, she would snap, "I did not more than I ought to do as a good Chicagoan."

She built one of the largest fountains in the world, the Buckingham Memorial Fountain in Chicago (seen at the opening of television's *Married with Children*). She dedicated it to the people of Chicago, in memory of her brother, to enhance Chicago's "front yard." During her life, she was called "Godmother to opera" and an art patron. She supported charities and charity cases. When she died in 1937, her will distributed $500,000 to her friends and relatives, and $126,000 to her maid, chauffeur, children of her caretaker, her nurses, doormen and elevator men at her Chicago residence. In 2007 dollars, that is over $8.9 million. That left $3.1 million, $40 million in 2007 dollars, for art and cultural organizations, including $2 million to the Chicago

Art Institute, $1 million to establish a memorial for Alexander Hamilton and $100,000 to maintain Buckingham Fountain.

After her death, Bald Head Farm was sold to Serge and Natalie Koussevitzky and renamed Seranak. The name was an acronym: Serge (Ser) and (a) Natalie (Na) Koussevitzky (K)—Seranak.

Koussevitzky was conductor of the Boston Symphony Orchestra. His dream was to establish a summer music festival and school. Tanglewood fulfilled that dream. In 1978, after the deaths of both the maestro and his wife, BSO purchased Seranak for $325,000. It became, by geography and sheer beauty, the crown of the Tanglewood grounds.

Today the grounds at Tanglewood Music Festival include approximately 500 acres combining three former Gilded Age estates: Tanglewood, Highwood and Seranak. The main campus—with the music shed, Ozawa Hall and a sea of parking—is roughly 330 contiguous acres that were Tanglewood and Highwood. The other 170 acres, across the road and up the hill, were Bald Hill Farm, then Seranak and now Tanglewood. If the gifts during her life and the bequests in her will are any indication, Kate would have been pleased. Tanglewood owes at least a nod, if not a doff of the hat, to two ladies from Pittsfield—Mrs. Coolidge and Miss Buckingham—who supported its beginnings and helped create its final shape.

AMERICA'S GILT COMPLEX

For more than a hundred years they have captured the interest of the American public. Their doings gave birth to the first society columns in American newspapers. They set the standard everyone wanted to emulate in clothes, domestic architecture, entertaining and lifestyle. They were, undisputedly, our first celebrities. To this day, we know their names; we catalogue their excesses; we laugh heartily at their foibles; and we cannot forget their contributions to American growth and culture. They were called robber barons, the Four Hundred, the economic aristocrats, the cottagers.

In the context of our governmental structure—our urge for freedom and equality—it may be thought that they would be resented. It may be thought that Americans resented the royal family they fought a revolution to oust. Neither seemed to be true—then and now America loved pomp and circumstance, grand economic display and the people who provided for it.

A select few material objects best represented the Gilded Age and made a clear statement about the economic superiority of the few. Foremost were the cottages themselves—the enormous architect-built country houses surrounded by manicured gardens, stables and greenhouses. A close second, however, was a much smaller object—a Charles Worth gown. Other smaller objects were exclusive to the very rich, such as decorative pieces made by Louis Comfort Tiffany, fans, flowers and jewels. Large or small, the objects all had one thing in common—in an age when a dollar a day was fair wage, these material goods cost thousands. The disproportionate cost symbolized the disproportionate distribution of wealth that was the defining characteristic of the age. The average man had to work and save every penny for a lifetime—making no expenditure for food, clothing or shelter—before he could afford a single material good. In short, they were beyond reach of the masses, but not beyond desire.

Evening gown, ca. 1900; ivory cut velvet over satin made by House of Worth, Paris, for Mrs. Evaline Kimball Salisbury of Chicago and Tor Court. *Photograph taken at the Berkshire Historical Society exhibition "Becoming Pittsfield." Courtesy of Gay Kimball Gamage and David Kimball.*

The father of haute couture, Charles Frederick Worth was born in England where he worked as a draper. In the mid-nineteenth century he moved to Paris to establish a dressmaking business called House of Worth. His gowns were intended for the queens of society and cost a king's ransom. A single Charles Worth gown cost thousands, putting them beyond the reach of the many. A Worth gown was distinguished by the highest quality fabrics and exceptional fit. A common practice among designers today, Charles Worth was the first to put his name in his clothes. The label represented the fact that Worth, as all future couturiers, considered his garments works of art.

Clothes spoke. A married woman's clothing expressed the economic status of her husband. The quality of the garment attested to her husband's wealth and position. At the height of Gilded Age excess, evening dresses were embossed with real gems—diamonds and pearls.

The color of evening clothes enunciated the woman's discretion and good taste, even her moral superiority. Muted shades, such as mauve, gray, black, ecru and white, were safe and distinguished. When Countess Olenska wore a red dress to a dinner party in Edith Wharton's *Age of Innocence*, she was committing a faux pas. When World War I ended, and women hiked up their skirts and added color with a vengeance, society ladies pronounced the Gilded Age over.

The social circuit of Gilded Age elite was prescribed just as were manners and dress. If one knew the rules, one went to Newport in summer, The Berkshires in fall, New York City in winter for the social season and Paris in spring to shop. While Paris remained the world's fashion capital, some Parisian couturiers established outlets in major American cities, such as New York. In addition, New York had its own designers and shops. The cachet of owning an evening dress from a French couturier, however, retained its significance throughout the Gilded Age.

As beautiful as a lady's garments were, they were equally impractical. The midriffs were tightly corseted, and Gilded Age ladies swooned not from faint hearts but from lack of oxygen. The hems dragged in mud and dust, pulling dirt in their wake.

Detail of the bodice of the Worth gown. *Photograph by Carole Owens.*

The shoes were featherweight, with leather soles as soft as gloves. Unfortunately for the wearer, they provided little support or comfort for the feet, however beautiful and elegant they might appear.

The children of the very rich were also meant to uphold the family honor by dressing to impress. *Godey's Lady's Book* proclaimed the Little Lord Fauntleroy suit "universally favored." It was inspired by the book of the same name published in 1886 and

written by English author Frances Burnett. The velvet suits were worn with broad-collared shirts and lace cuffs.[17] This suit was made by Hollander and Co., an elite clothing retailer in the late nineteenth century with stores in Boston, Newport and Paris. Hollander and Co. provided clothes for both adults and children.

As a young man Louis Comfort Tiffany (1848–1933) studied to be a painter, and one of his tutors was George Inness. In

Boy's suit, ca. 1900; navy blue velvet, satin and leather with label from L.P. Hollander and Co., Boston. Three-piece boy's suit worn by member of the Allen family. *Courtesy of Alice R. Olcott, descendent of the Allen family.*

the 1870s, however, he decided to create his pictures, not in paint, but in glass. He developed methods for the creation of opalescent glass, glass in many colors and Favrile, the iridescent glass he patented in 1880.

In 1885 he founded the Tiffany Glass Company in conjunction with his father's store Tiffany & Co. The Tiffany brand was lifted from commercial enterprise to purveyor of fine arts. His iridescent glass products became synonymous with good taste and fine craftsmanship. The Tiffany factory made art glass, jewelry, silver, cloth and cabinets. The products were coveted all over the world.

The Tiffany Glass & Decorating Company, founded in 1892, was an American tastemaker. The sheer multiplicity of Tiffany decorative objects, their wide distribution and high level of craftsmanship, influenced America's definition of beauty.

The high price of Tiffany objects created a market for imitation, and Riviere Studios was one of the most prolific imitators. Since the demand was strong and the price prohibitive, there were copies of all the precious ornamentation found in Berkshire cottages. William and John Sloane created W.J. Sloane Company based on copies of oriental rugs, Sheridan desks and Queen Anne chairs.

However, there were things that could not be imitated; things that had to be learned inside the inner circle. The Gilded Age was not just the birth of the gossip or society column, but also of a spate of books on manners and entertaining. The granddaughter of a prominent cottager said, "I could tell as the person approached if they were a member of our social circle. It was the clothes, you see." If for any reason the clothes deceived, then, "I could tell the moment they opened their mouths."

There was an in-group pronunciation that could be heard, years later, when Franklin Delano Roosevelt delivered his fireside chats or Eleanor spoke out on a favorite issue. And yet... Edith Wharton wrote that it was *deplaisante*, "displeasing," for a lady to say precisely what she meant in Gilded Age society. Verbal speech was subtle, indirect and supplemented by the "languages" of inanimate objects. Here is a brief "dictionary" of the language of the fan:

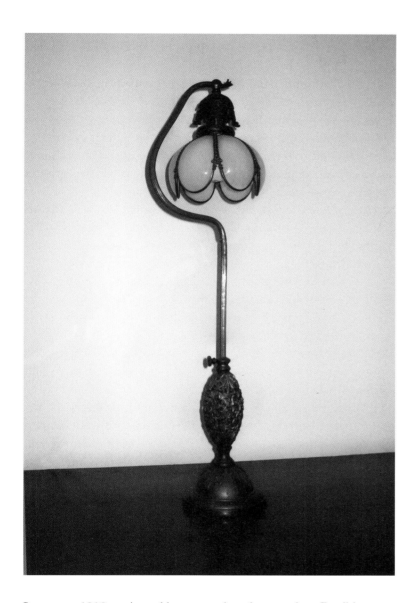

Lamp, ca. 1910; patinated bronze and opalescent glass. Possibly made by Tiffany; owned by the Kimball family. *Courtesy of Gay Kimball Gamage and David Kimball.*

Rest the fan on your lips: *I do not trust you.*
Allow a closed fan to dangle from left hand: *I am engaged.*
Allow a closed fan to dangle from right hand: *I am available.*
Place a half-open fan over face: *Someone is listening.*
Open fan to fullest point, avert eyes and stare at it: *I like you.*
Quickly, sharply close fan: *I am not pleased.*

It was said that a true lady never said exactly what she meant. Perhaps because subtlety was prized over clarity in verbal communication, many objects were invested with symbolic meaning. Chief among these wordless messengers were the clothes on your back, but a favorite of young ladies and lovers were flowers.

Different species of flowers represented different words that could be combined into secret messages. To communicate accurately, however, one had to be able to differentiate between subtle shades:

A white lily: *It is heaven being with you.*
A yellow lily: *I am walking on air.*
An orange lily: *I hate you.*

Furthermore, the message changed if the senders and recipients were men or women:

Camellia, woman to man: *Good luck.*
Camellia, man to woman: *Expressing admiration for your perfection.*
White carnation, man to woman: *Good luck.*

Combining flowers also created a message:

Red rose surrounded by fern: *I am sincere in my love for you.*
Rich display of purple hyacinth and yellow jonquil: *I am sorry, please forgive me.*

Although the watercolor of Tor Court shown in the photograph on the following page was produced by Hillcrest

Watercolor of Tor Court interior used as a Christmas card, 1949.
Courtesy of Gail Pinna.

photographers were hired by the cottagers to produce cards like these for use as invitations or holiday greetings. Alternatively, companies like the Detroit Publishing Company photographed the estates from the road and produced souvenir postcards for sale to the public.

In 1902, shortly after the Reverend R. DeWitt Mallary's book, *Lenox and the Berkshire Highlands,* was published, a reporter for *Lenox Life* ravaged the book. Was it ill-written, poorly researched or morally offensive? No. Mallary had not insulted the cottagers; he had simply slighted their worth. "Faint praise of the summer dwellers is not enough," the reporter wrote with heat.

Mallary had praised earlier Pittsfield dwellers Oliver Wendell Holmes and Herman Melville, and Stockbridge dweller Nathaniel Hawthorne, more highly than the cottagers.

It is an undeniable fact that the social prestige of the people who own the country places today is quite as high as that of those highly intellectual people. The men and women who own the beautiful estates, who have spent vast sums of money beautifying them, deserve better.

There was a national love for wealth, display and those who provided it. There was even public approbation for the accumulation and dispensation of wealth over the accumulation and dispensation of knowledge. The reporter concluded that in Mallary's book, it was "a little tiresome to have that ancient history and those [literary] people referred to so often."

Hospital as a Christmas card, it is in the tradition of cottage stationery. When a cottage was completed, the madam sent announcements to her circle of friends—cards with a painting or photograph of the house. Hostesses placed stationery with a line drawing of the house or with the name of the house embossed on the letterhead in each guest bedroom. Artists or

GILDED AGE PHILANTHROPY

What's that? You thought the Gilded Age was all about greed. Grasping for fortunes and spending lavishly on self-fulfillment if not self-aggrandizement.

One cannot deny that in a time when a house could be built for $1,000 to $2,000, the Gilded Age elite spent hundreds of thousands on a second home; when one could run up a dress for the cost of the yardage, a Worth gown cost thousands. Nonetheless, in 1889 Andrew Carnegie wrote *The Gospel of Wealth*, expressing his belief that it was the obligation of the wealthy to give. He called it noblesse oblige, and wrote, "To die rich is to die in disgrace."[18]

Philanthropy was born with mankind. Harvard claims that the first recorded fund drive in the New World was on campus in the mid-seventeenth century. Harvard was seven years old, and they raised money for a scholarship fund—£500. Still it was during the Gilded Age that philanthropy took the form it has now, and our modern practice of eleemosynary giving was perfected in the Gilded Age. Following are a few examples of Berkshire cottagers who made substantive contributions.

The contributions of the Allen family to Pittsfield helped establish the town as a transportation and cultural center and ultimately led to it becoming the city of Pittsfield.

Abraham Burbank arrived in Pittsfield a young man with little money and modest prospects as a clerk. When he died in 1887, his estate was valued at $350,000 (about $6 million in 2007 dollars). He left the bulk of his estate to the town of Pittsfield for schools, hospitals and parks.

From 1881 through the turn of the century, Morris K. Jesup of Belvoir Terrace presided over the Museum of Natural History's golden age, enlarging the facility and funding the Perry expedition to the North Pole and the Jesup expedition to the Northern Pacific.

In 1887 Emily Vanderbilt Sloane of Elm Court founded the Sloane Maternity Hospital (Columbia University Medical Center Department of Obstetrics today). The Astor, Morgan and Vanderbilt families founded the Metropolitan Opera House, as well as several museums. The economic elite of the Gilded Age changed the cultural landscape of America with their generosity. So widespread was their giving and so complete their impact that the Gilded Age has been called the American Renaissance.

Carnegie, Rockefeller and banking heiress Margaret Olivia Slocum Sage established the nation's first foundations dedicated to improving American society. Rockefeller's foundation helped wipe out some diseases and is credited with funding the initial research that finally led to the discovery of DNA. Baltimore merchant Johns Hopkins donated $7 million to establish a hospital and university in his name. In addition to their contributions to culture and education, the Gilded Age millionaires made a significant contribution to American health and welfare. They built the first orphanages.

But, you might ask, was it all beer and skittles, gas and gators? How could we have been so wrong? What about the greedy, spendthrift robber barons?

Here's the conundrum. Putting his money where his mouth was, Carnegie gave away 90 percent of his wealth to charitable causes. By the time Carnegie died in 1919, he had given away $350 million. That is approximately $7 billion in today's dollars. The money built twenty-five hundred public libraries, which were credited with raising the country's literacy rate. Carnegie also funded schools and universities—all, he stated, for the common good. Yet a few short years later, for the common good, Andrew Carnegie fired his superintendent of grounds because he asked for a raise from $60 per month to $70 per month. If you can understand why Carnegie gave away millions but denied an employee an additional $120 per year, you can understand the beating heart of the Gilded Age. You are at the core of the philosophy, politics and philanthropy of the moneyed and powerful.

Here is a clue: it wasn't about the money. Writing in 1851, Hawthorne explained it succinctly, "I prefer a small right than a large favor." A gift is not an entitlement. Voluntary giving is not regulated. The Gilded Age economic elite, Carnegie included, were willing to share wealth, not power—to donate to their fellow citizens, not entitle them to a more even distribution of wealth.

GILDED AGE PERFIDY

Pittsfield, August 20, 1900, 2:37 a.m.—Charley Poole pumps as hard and fast as he can. It is about a mile from 287 Tyler Street to Circular Avenue where he must sound the alarm. Not exactly Paul Revere, Charlie is a journalistic legman. His job is to ride or run like the wind from the site of a big news story to the home or office of a newshawk (reporter). If he gets there first, if the story is a good one, Charlie could earn a dime or as much as a dollar. Like any of his competitors in the trade, Charlie is a lad, but on this night he is way ahead of the pack. He has a bicycle, and he has a lantern. It is black, dark and moonless, and while Pittsfield has street lighting—over thirteen hundred lamps with twenty-five candlepower each—they are not on.

"Why," Charley wonders, not for the first time, "do the city fathers see fit to turn off the electric streetlights at 12:30 a.m.?" Sure, Charley knows what they say—decent folk have no business on the streets after midnight. "But," Charley thinks as he swerves to avoid the wooden horses that block freshly paved sections of North Street, "I am decent, and I have very important business."

Charley holds the lantern higher in one hand and skids into the turn on Linden Avenue, thinking the lantern was a lucky find. It will later be suggested that he nicked the back of Dr. Frank K. Paddock's carriage with the lantern, but at the moment it is worth it. Charley pumps as hard and fast as he can...he is going to be first with the story.

As Charley ponders the decisions of his elders, Dr. Paddock is pacing in front of 287 Tyler with a question of his own. "How dare they have called for the police and a doctor and then bade them wait, and wait, before allowing them to enter the house?"

Finally, as Charles skids onto Circular Avenue and stops at the newshawk's house, he hears the citywide alarm go off. It is the fire bell, but when folks neither see nor smell smoke, they will know to go to the police station. At the police station Chief Nicholson and Captain White pass out firearms commandeered from the local hardware store and the hunt is on. "Wake up!" Charley shouts. "Wake up! It's murder! A murder has been done!"

When the story broke, it was very big: the daughter of a prominent Pittsfield family had been murdered in her bedroom. Three hundred Pittsfield men gathered at the police station in answer to the fire alarm and were assigned routes to search. They were looking for two or three masked men who broke into the R.L. Fosburg home on Tyler Street shortly after 1:00 a.m. They entered as thieves, fought with Mr. Robert Fosburg and his son Robert S. Fosburg, shot wildly, hitting daughter Miss May Fosburg, and ran from the scene as murderers. The posse searched for two days as far north as Williamstown, west to the state line, east to Cummington and south to Lenox.

Theories ran through Berkshire County faster than the posse. Mr. Fosburg had been hired by the Stanley Works to oversee operations and construction of a new plant in Morningside. It was well known that cash money to pay salaries was carried down North Street and sometimes stowed in the Fosburg home until the day wages were paid out. Perhaps the thieves knew that too, and they were there to rob the payroll. On the other hand, there had been a robbery at a house in Springfield a few days before. Perhaps there was a gang roaming the area waiting to pounce on unsuspecting householders. Governor W. Murray Crane brought in the Pinkertons. Mr. Fosburg offered $1,500 for information, and the City of Pittsfield matched it. Yet no suspects were arrested, and the mystery deepened. The clues, a shoe and a few footprints, had the oddest way of leading, not away from the Fosburg house, but back to it. Chief Nicholson took a second look.

Dr. Paddock could not fix the time of death any more precisely than between 10:00 p.m. on August 19 and 2:00 a.m. on August 20. The neighbors heard two pistol shots at 2:00 a.m. and called for the police. Nicholson brought the doctor, and then that odd wait occurred of almost thirty minutes while the Fosburgs denied access to the house. When they entered, Nicholson and Paddock found May Fosburg dead from a gunshot wound just outside a second floor bedroom. The witnesses, Mr. and Mrs.

Wendell Hotel Tap Room. *Courtesy of the Berkshire Athenaeum.*

Robert Fosburg and their son and daughter-in-law, Mr. and Mrs. Robert S. Fosburg, all clung to the story of the masked intruders. Yet Nicholson traced the shoe to a purchase made by the elder Mr. Fosburg.

City newshawks congregated at the Tap Room of the Wendell Hotel. It had a separate entrance on West Street, a men's club atmosphere and good liquor. When the story of the murder broke, reporters came to Pittsfield from all over the United States and Europe. With a nose for news and an instinct for newsmen's hangouts, they all registered at the Wendell.

Built in 1898, the Wendell was on a scale and level of adornment never seen in Pittsfield, and evidently not appreciated. The builder, Samuel W. Bowerman, was only twenty-three years old. Obviously an ambitious man with a flair, he did not understand the Pittsfield market. Six months after the Wendell was completed, Bowerman was out of business. The Wendell was then leased to a management firm, but by 1900, it was not certain they could make a go of it. Then came the night of August 20, 1900. Reporters arrived in Pittsfield to cover the story. Possibly because they were city men and appreciated the fancy digs;

The Wendell Hotel. *Courtesy of the Berkshire Athenaeum.*

definitely because of the proximity to the courthouse and the telegraph office, they all chose the Wendell. There, just eight months into the new century, they took out their notebooks and typewriters, set to work and proclaimed the Fosburg murder "the crime of the century."

The investigation dragged on. Nicholson found no trace of a gang or any outsiders. The four witnesses appeared to him to be the four suspects. It troubled him that in addition to the dead sister, the younger Fosburg's wife had a torn nightdress and a marked face. Further investigation caused him to arrest the victim's brother, Robert S.

The family stood firm in their story, and the gentry from the governor to the cottagers stood behind them. The trial did not take place until July 1901. After the case for the prosecution was presented, the judge dismissed the jury and found that the state presented insufficient evidence to convict. Robert S. Fosburg was released.

Through it all, the Wendell remained full and bustling. When Robert S. was arrested (and released on his own recognizance), he left the Tyler Street house and took up residence at the Wendell alone. When Robert S. was acquitted, the celebration took place at the Wendell. The case was never officially solved. The search for justice and closure was thwarted, but the odd and unintended outcome of the trial was that the Wendell Hotel was saved from financial failure.

AMERICA'S SECOND GILDED AGE?

In both positive and negative ways, commentators theorize that this is America's second Gilded Age. Working from the definition of the Gilded Age as a time when vast new wealth was created and disproportionately distributed, they point to the Internet and the technology revolution. They cite a corporate report that states the chief operation officer (CEO) earned $3 million per year while an employee in the same corporation earned $40,000. They point out that as the salaries of the CEOs rise into the millions annually, the newly minted billionaires spend millions on thirty-thousand-square-foot homes, hundreds of thousands on parties and a reported $60,000 on a single shower curtain. They quote laws and regulations whereby every avenue for employees to sue the corporation for unfair employment practices are being blocked by legislation and consent agreements. They identify this as an attempt to undo the post-Gilded Age safety net: social security, unemployment insurance and workers' rights.

Without doubt the national transportation system was a product of the Gilded Age, and huge natural resources could be moved to manufacturer and then to market. More people worked outside the home, stores were more accessible and homespun gave way to a desire for store-bought. Our national wealth was more dependent upon consumption of manufactured goods, and the definition of "the people" shifted from citizens to consumers—the value of the people to the economic and political powers was more as consumers than as voters.

Those who believe this is a second Gilded Age point out that the redefinition of "we the people" as consumers has persisted from that day to this, and in one of the nation's darkest hours, after September 11, our elected officials asked the public to shop. Furthermore, they say if history and civics classes cease to be taught in the schools at the same time as vending machines are rolled into the hallways, are we teaching our children to be better citizens or better consumers? They mention that the number of minutes of advertising on radio and television relative to the minutes of programming has tripled. At the same time, educational programming has decreased and fewer Americans vote at the polls. They believe these things echo the first Gilded Age and fear that people will forget that citizens are equal in the voting booth, but never equal at the emporium.

Others disagree and say the Gilded Age was significantly different in several ways. They point out that there was no income tax during the Gilded Age. The ability to raise funds through taxation strengthened the government. In turn government became something it had not been in the Gilded Age—a provider of services to the masses.

The population of the United States grew from fifty million to seventy-six million during the Gilded Age. Opponents cite the current population of the United States—three hundred million. Larger populations create a strain on resources and problems of governance previously unknown.

Further, they say the expenditures of the Gilded Age elite were not all frivolous and self-indulgent. Prior to the Gilded Age, America was viewed much as a third world country is viewed today. Some of the spending was to establish the United States as a nation that deserved a place at the international table— a nation of culture, taste, manners and discrimination. The Gilded Age elite copied the style and the "civilized" ways of the Europeans. The United States, today, has a place at the head of the international table and expects other nations to emulate it.

In the Gilded Age, the new mobility drove change. The train, the trolley and the automobile made fortunes for the owners and enhanced the lifestyles of the consumers. The single underpinning of it all was the new fuel-based economy. Oil and gas consumption born in the Gilded Age is maturing, aging and perhaps dying in our time. Those who do not think this is a second Gilded Age say the fuel-based economy born in the Gilded Age may die in this century.

Real enlightenment probably comes, not from determining which side is right, but from understanding the points made by each.

In the year 1905, the average life expectancy was forty-seven years. The total number of murders in the United States was 230. Only 14 percent of American homes had a bathtub; 8 percent had a telephone, while 18 percent had at least one domestic servant. There were 8,000 cars in America, and only 144 miles of paved roads. An accountant and an engineer earned about $2,000 per year. An estimated 90 percent of doctors did not attend college; they attended medical schools similar to trade schools that taught techniques. More Americans believed in the efficacy of a séance than an anesthetic. Approximaely 95 percent of births took place at home, and 2 out of every 10 Americans were illiterate. Marijuana, cocaine and heroin were sold by pharmacies as "perfect guardians of health." The most common causes of death were pneumonia, influenza and tuberculosis. White-collar, blue-collar or gilt-edged life was different one hundred years ago.

History may repeat itself, but when it does, the context has changed.

PART II

THE GEM CITY

INTRODUCING PITTSFIELD

Pittsfield was incorporated as a town in 1761 with a population of 428. The basis of the Pittsfield economy was agriculture, and it seemed it would develop in the same way as other Berkshire villages. Yet one man, the Reverend Thomas Allen, knew that was not true. He said Pittsfield would grow into an industrial city. Actually, he was more observant than prescient. Before his death in 1810, the carders, millers and manufacturers had come to Pittsfield. The wool makers, clock and gun makers, smiths and tanners soon followed.

By 1865, the beginning of the Gilded Age, Pittsfield grew to eleven thousand strong—almost thirty times its founding population. By 1890 the population was 17,281. By 1917, the end of the Gilded Age, Pittsfield was a city of 39,607; a population almost one hundred times larger than it was at incorporation, bustling with train and trolley travel, industry and culture.

During the Gilded Age the Pittsfield carders and sheep breeders, millers, tanners and gun and wool makers were no longer dominant, and many of their manufactories were retooled. Pittsfield became home to manufacturers of the modern age: makers of electricity, trucks and automobiles, the paper for United States currency and fine writing paper for an increasingly well-educated populace.

As industry grew, jobs were created. As jobs were created, more people came to Pittsfield to earn a wage. As wages increased, there was "a bit extra for store-bought" and North Street shops multiplied. Homes and parks were built, and the civic buildings were rebuilt in a manner more befitting a growing and prosperous town. Pittsfield was not merely the geographic center of Berkshire County, but also the center of transportation and commerce.

The transformation of Pittsfield from a country town to a city was reflected in the buildings. South Street, lined with clapboard homes and Elm trees, became a cultural center with the erection of the Berkshire Museum and the Colonial Theater. Park Square,

Park Square, looking west. *Courtesy of the Berkshire Athenaeum.*

reminiscent of many New England town squares with gracious homes, a few shops and the church, became the center of civic responsibility and culture with the building of the county courthouse and the Athenaeum. The clearest symbol of Pittsfield's prosperity, however, was the homes—the gracious homes of Pittsfield's resident millionaires and the Berkshire cottages.

Pittsfield was growing on the back of industry. Its rural aspects were shrinking. The Gilded Age resorts were usually places of uncompromised beauty. Gilded Age economic elite were content to derive their fortunes from manufactories and refineries that marred the landscape and created fetid air, but they were not willing to build in sight of them. How, then, did the Gilded Age economic elite create a colony in Pittsfield?

In an age when it was believed that mountain air was a restorative, Pittsfield was one of the highest points in Berkshire County. The trip from Lenox and Stockbridge to Pittsfield was straight uphill. Pittsfield's city center was on a plateau at fourteen hundred feet above sea level. The manufactories were built in the valleys, hidden from the gracious shopping streets, parks and residential areas. The estates built along the lakes and tucked into residential neighborhoods were far from the industry that brought prosperity.

Pittsfield differed from other Gilded Age resorts in many ways. The cottagers were from Chicago, not New York, and some but not all cottages had names. The reason was simple. In Lenox and Stockbridge there were no house numbers—that is, no addresses—and a house name was mandatory to identify its location. Pittsfield was much larger and had addresses, rendering a house name optional. These small differences paled in light of the one significant difference between Pittsfield and other resorts.

In Lenox and Stockbridge, the cottagers bought a dozen farms to stitch together one estate of five hundred to seven hundred acres. As the price of land rose from $5 to $50 to $500 per acre, farmers sold their land, and the agriculturally based economy disappeared. Many farmers went to work on the estates. Slowly a cottage economy was created. The village of Lenox, with a population of a few thousand, became dependent on the cottagers for their livelihood. Residents lived year-round on the money they earned in the three summer months. Pittsfield's economy was based upon industry in the valley, shops at city center and transportation throughout the town. The presence of a vibrant middle class and an entrenched upper middle class kept Pittsfield rooted in its own identity and invulnerable to an economic takeover by the cottagers.

In 1872 it was first suggested by Thomas F. Plunkett that Pittsfield become a city. The suggestion, made at the April town meeting, fell flat. No one supported it. Townsfolk were not interested. It took seventeen years for the town meeting to vote in the affirmative, and nineteen years to become the city of Pittsfield.

The criterion to become a city was a population minimum followed by a mandatory two-year waiting period. Pittsfield's growth was obvious and exponential—what then was the objection? In *The History of Pittsfield*, Edward Boltwood wrote that "Pittsfield's traditional and deeply rooted repugnance to the delegation of authority" was the root of the problem.[19] Citizens of Pittsfield were opposed to becoming a city because they would lose the cornerstone of democracy, the greatest right of the people—the vote.

In a Massachusetts town, every citizen could attend the town meeting and vote on every issue. If a town became a city, it changed from a pure democracy to a representative democracy with a mayor and town council. Rather than vote on every issue of town governance, citizens would be able to vote only once to choose their representatives. The vote and direct political involvement were important. As Samuel Bowerman stated, "I should rather vote to build a new town hall seating 5,000 people than vote to surrender the present right of every citizen to engage actively in the affairs of the town."[20]

In 1891, when Pittsfield had a population of over thirty-nine thousand, and had grown from ninety streets to four hundred streets, from two thousand private residences to over six thousand, the idea of becoming a city was finally accepted; or more accurately, the enormous growth finally overpowered the opposition. There was also a change in attitude.

Pittsfield was a microcosm of the changing attitudes across America during the Gilded Age. The redefinition of the people as consumers accelerated and at the same time voting was cheapened. Even in Pittsfield the rhetoric changed. At a Monday evening club meeting, the speaker railed:

The future growth of Pittsfield depends upon the increase of manufacturing. One large factory would do more for permanent prosperity of this town than our new courthouse or another town meeting.

In 1891 Pittsfield became a city—the first city in Berkshire County. In 1893, in an excess of zeal, a writer described the new city: "Pittsfield is as fashionable as New York, as progressive as Chicago, as conservative as Philadelphia, and as literary as Boston…just smaller."

Even though the "representative businessmen of Pittsfield" were paying the writer to wax rhapsodic, Pittsfield did have a great deal of which to be proud. Its transformation from country town to city was not in name only. Pittsfield was big and brawny with industry, bustling with commercial energy and vibrant with goods and entertainment. It was the county seat with a fine courthouse and its own Athenaeum.

Pittsfield's millionaires were homegrown and civic-minded. They were not wealthy industrialists who arrived at apple blossom (May) and deserted at apple drop (September). The Pittsfield millionaires were permanent residents who supported and invested in their city. With a fortunate topography and intelligent planning, manufactories were hidden in the lowland, leaving center city clean and attractive to residents, tourists and cottagers. It was a popular destination for county residents and outlanders because of its beauty and culture. Pittsfield was a jewel.

A 1905 pamphlet printed by Sun Publishing and paid for by Berkshire Life Insurance Company of Pittsfield summed it up: "Pittsfield's fame is wide spread and the term 'Gem City' by which it is known, is most fittingly applied."

A gem is anything prized for its beauty, especially if it is both small and beautiful. Furthermore, a gem, like Pittsfield, had facets: the natural beauty, mountain air and pure drinking water of the country enhanced by the fire department, sewage system, electrified streets and multiple goods, services and entertainments found in cities. Pittsfield was smaller than Philadelphia, New York and Chicago, geographically removed from their congestion and noise, but still accessible.

GETTING THERE

The prosperity of Pittsfield was no accident. The visionaries of Pittsfield made three decisions that presaged the coming boom. In the 1860s the city fathers fought to bring the county seat from Lenox to Pittsfield; in the 1880s, they brought William Stanley to Pittsfield and underwrote his experiments with electricity; and predating both, in 1834, they began their fight to bring the railroad into Pittsfield.

Everyone loved The Berkshires, but admitted that, in any direction, they were next door to nowhere. Fifty miles from any port, 135 miles from New York or Boston, in a time when travel was on horseback or by stagecoach, The Berkshires were an easy distance from nowhere. What brought The Berkshires closer to the Chicago cottagers and vacationers from Albany, New York, and Connecticut was the railroad.

Gilded Age economics were simple with a cruel finality—if you were on the railroad line your town grew and prospered; if you were not, it shriveled and died. The businessmen of Pittsfield knew that. The first train pulled into Berkshire County in 1838, but not into Pittsfield. Business interests in town wanted Pittsfield to be not just on the line but the hub of Berkshire transportation. The battle was waged between Pittsfield in Central County and the villages in south Berkshire County.

Lee, Lenox and Stockbridge in South County asserted that they provided the most direct route into the county from Hudson, Albany and Connecticut. Pittsfield took care to send its best men to Boston to dispute the point. Of course the Pittsfield men claimed the most direct route was Albany to Pittsfield. In bald fact, the difference in distance was sixty-six one-hundredths of a mile. The real difference was in grade—there were five summits on the southern route and only four on the northern route, and the average grade favored the northern route. Estimates indicated the southern route was about $32,000 cheaper to lay, but still the engineers favored the more northern route and supported Pittsfield.

Union Station. *Courtesy of Berkshire Historical Society.*

Supporters of the southern route argued valiantly, and even asked for a postponement until the following year, hoping to find their own engineers. But on June 15, 1837, Pittsfield won. The *Pittsfield Sun* reported victory and called for a salute to be fired in the town square. The *Sun*'s glee was understandable since early subscribers of the railroad were *Sun* editor Phinehas Allen and his brother Jonathan, father of the future railroad man and cottager Thomas Allen.

By 1840 the first train had arrived in Pittsfield from Albany. By 1842, an advertisement jubilantly exclaimed that the train, traveling an average twenty-five miles per hour, made the trip in less than two hours.

To understand what the excitement was about, compare that trip to a newspaper report about General Lafayette's visit from Albany to Pittsfield in 1825. Lafayette left Albany on horseback at 6:00 a.m. He arrived in Lebanon Springs at 2:30 p.m., eight hours later. He changed to a coach, and at 6:00 p.m., he arrived at the Merrick Coffee House next to the Bullfinch Church in the center of Pittsfield. The trip took twelve hours.

Similarly, an 1837 stagecoach advertisement in the *Hartford Courant* read:

Safe pleasant and expeditious traveling...Through by daylight...
Leave the United States Hotel at 4 o'clock a.m. (Sundays excepted)

The interior of Union Station. This is the second Union Station built in Pittsfield. *Courtesy of Berkshire Scenic Railway Museum, Arthur Nichols Collection.*

and arrive in Albany at 7 ½ p.m. The coaches are new strong and easy in motion, and every care has been taken to procure careful obliging and steady drivers.

Thus "expeditious travel" from Hartford to Albany, before the train, took fifteen and a half hours.

Just as the airplane would shrink the planet, the train moved Berkshire County hours closer to ports and major population centers. Time was not the only consideration—the journey itself was more pleasant by train. A stagecoach was cramped, and the roadway uncertain. The words in the coach ad "through by daylight" were seriously meant. It was better to arrange to leave at 4:00 a.m. than to risk the danger of a stagecoach ride over rough road in the dark. On the other hand, according to the *Pittsfield Sun* in July 1843:

The (train) cars for passengers…were large, roomy, and well-ventilated, about 50 feet in length, fitted up with separate stuffed mahogany chairs…for the 80 passengers.

The reporter extolled the view from the window, and "the stillness and unjarring steadiness" of the ride. All this compared to the wheels of the stage bumping over root and rock outcroppings on narrow roads. Stagecoach travel fought for survival against the iron horse, and lost. As train travel was faster, travelers could go farther. As it was more comfortable, the journey was viewed as part of the vacation.

Tourists could come from the cities for the country air. Pittsfield could move its manufactured goods to far-flung markets anywhere in the country. Travel within the county was also facilitated. Berkshire County was a rectangle with its longest side running north and south. The distance from the southernmost to the northernmost end of the county was equal to the trip from Albany to Pittsfield. Stockbridge and Lenox licked their wounds and swiftly laid track north to connect to the Pittsfield hub.

It would be hard to think of many things that affected the economic development of Berkshire County more than the arrival of the train.

THE PITTSFIELD PRESS

Thursday, March 5, 1868, was an odd day for Phinehas Allen. The task he set for himself was equivalent to writing his own obituary.

Phinehas Allen was the nephew of "the Fighting parson." He arrived in Pittsfield in 1800. Allen had apprenticed at a newspaper, the *Hampshire Gazette*, and at twenty-four years old, was confident he could establish his own newspaper. He called it the *Pittsfield Sun*. The commitment to objectivity associated with modern journalism was not felt in 1800. Allen loudly and proudly proclaimed the *Sun* to be the voice of the Democratic Party. In 1829, his son, Phinehas, joined the staff.

On March 5, 1868, under the headline "Destructive Fire in Pittsfield," Allen wrote of the complete destruction of the *Sun* offices:

> *Today, for the first time in more than sixty-seven years, the* Pittsfield Sun *does not appear precisely on the date announced…and some of our subscribers may fail to receive their papers this week.*

In the early morning hours of Wednesday, March 4, 1868, the night watchman employed by W.M. Root to guard the Root Block on North Street saw smoke. The Root Block housed the United States Post Office, Joseph Gregory's Clothing Store, the Oliver Root Boot and Shoe Store, W.M. Root's Silver and Jewelry Store, the Berkshire Life Insurance Company, the dental office of Dr. Clark Hall, the medical office of Dr. F.A. Cady, dressmaker Miss Rosa Hatch, tailor Joseph Gregory, tobacconist Theron Streeter, the dwelling of J.D. Kennedy and Allen's beloved *Sun* printing office and bookstore.

It was just after 2:00 a.m. in the bitter cold when the watchman roused Mr. Kennedy, who barely had time to escape, and sounded the alarm. When the firemen arrived, they found that the water in the tank (hydrant) closest to Root

North Street, Pittsfield. *Courtesy of the Berkshire Athenaeum.*

Block was frozen solid. The next closest tank was absolutely dry. Firemen scrambled to melt frozen water and to search as far as Park Square to find a full tank. All the while, fire licked the walls and ignited the roof. It was a long time before a stream of water hit the flames. It seemed certain the block would be a total loss; all the businesses burned out; personal investments and lifelong savings gone up in smoke. Fear that every building from Park to School Street would soon ignite swept through the firefighters and the crowd of onlookers. The article Phinehas Allen wrote on the morning of March 5 told of damage estimated at $75,000, almost $1.8 million in today's dollars—the biggest fire in Pittsfield's history.

Yet on that frigid morning, with flames the only light, the citizens of Pittsfield did not stand idly by. When the *Sun* went to press, the story was one of tragedy and triumph, sorrow and gratitude.

The firemen did not take a break. More and more came forward to volunteer to man the hoses and produce a steady stream of water for no less than four hours. The Herculean effort limited the damage to the Root Block. Colonel Robert Pomeroy and Mrs. Edwin Clapp arranged refreshments and gallons of hot coffee for everyone who came to help. Pittsfield men and women formed squads and braved the flames. They went in and out of the burning building, successfully removing most of Mr. Root's stock of jewelry, all of the mail from the post office, small safes in more than one office that held the cash savings of their neighbors and, as the fire smoldered and died, the almost five-hundred-pound safe from the Berkshire Life Insurance office. As soon as dawn broke, businesses untouched by the tragedy opened their doors to those afflicted. The post office opened for business close to the regular hour in the Berkshire Block on West Street beside the Merchant's Union Express office. The Old Western Massachusetts Insurance Office welcomed its competitor, Berkshire Life, into its offices.

It was Chickering, Axtell and Durkee of the *Berkshire Evening Eagle* who, with "careful and practiced hands," removed all the type and printing material from the *Sun* office.

The men of the *Eagle* returned to their offices and composed the following message:

> *P. Allen, Esq. We take the earliest opportunity to tender to you any facilities we have in our office to enable you to go on with your printing business, and get out your paper. Please make free to occupy room and use such material and facilities in our office that you need. With sympathy for you in your misfortune, and congratulating you that everything was not destroyed, we remain very truly yours.*

On the front page of the *Sun*, Allen replied "We are personally under obligation (and) acknowledge gratefully the fraternal courtesies which [the *Eagle*] offered."

It was not, after all, the obituary of the *Sun*—the *Sun* was published in Pittsfield continuously for 106 years. However, in May 1868, only two months after the fire, Phinehas Allen the elder died. He died having witnessed the heart of Pittsfield—a city of brave citizens and good neighbors, who in adversity suspended all competition.

THE PITTSFIELD MILLIONAIRES

The permanent residents of Pittsfield were amassing wealth from local industry that resulted in primary homes of beauty and architectural importance equal to the cottages of the Gilded Age elite. These homes represented more than individual wealth. They reflected a stable economy that prevented the Pittsfield population from becoming dependent on a seasonal cottager economy. Furthermore, the presence of a healthy middle class and growing upper class anchored the city and its identity in the products of its own enterprise—not shaped by individuals who made their money elsewhere and only spent it in The Berkshires. Therefore the homes shown in the photographs are beautiful to look at and important to understanding Pittsfield during the Gilded Age.

Charles Whittlesey was born in 1869, the second son of Elihu Whittlesey, a Pittsfield mill superintendent. In 1872 the third and last child, a sister, was born. In 1874 his mother Mary Smith Whittlesey died. When Charles was ten years old, his father remarried. Elihu and Isabel Axtell Whittlesey decided to keep and raise two-year-old daughter Mary, but not the two sons. It was arranged that a childless Pittsfield couple named Power would adopt Charles and his twelve-year-old brother Theodore. Charles became Charles Whittlesey Power. It was perhaps an unusual story and may have generated questions and comments, but whatever the motivations, it ended well. The boys went to a loving and financially stable home and thrived. Whittlesey Power was president of the Third National Bank and Trust Company, mayor of Pittsfield and chairman of the Pittsfield Community Chest. The most important indication of his reaction to the adoption was that, throughout his life, he used the double last name—accepting his adopted parents and never rejecting his natural father.

Arthur Eaton's idea that fine stationary could be produced in Pittsfield was a very successful one. Eaton Hurlbut (later Eaton & Pike) was the second largest employer in town. After

Whittlesey Power Home. *Courtesy of the Berkshire Athenaeum.*

William A. Whittlesey House. *Courtesy of the Berkshire Athenaeum.*

Bishop Worthington House. *Courtesy of the Berkshire Athenaeum.*

the marriage of his daughter Ethel to Winthrop Murray Crane, the company became Eaton, Crane & Pike. Eaton's house was on South Street.

Eaton's son remained in Pittsfield, an Eaton, Crane & Pike employee, and built his home on South Street near his father's house. In 1925, at Pittsfield's St. Stephens Church, his daughter Isabel married Kimball Salisbury and became a resident of Tor Court and Chicago.

W.A. Whittlesey (no relation to Elihu Whittlesey) arrived in Pittsfield at a propitious moment for a man of his interests and

abilities. It was in 1886, the year Stanley tested his theory of alternating current in Great Barrington.

In 1890 Whittlesey effected the amalgamation of Pittsfield Illuminating Company and the Stanley Electrical Company and created the Pittsfield Electric Company. From his first day in Pittsfield to his last, he promoted the company and sold its wares, easing the transition to an electrified Pittsfield.

If the definition of a cottage was a second home built during the Gilded Age with no less than twenty rooms on no less than thirty acres, and the Thomas Colt house was built as a primary

Colt Joslin House. *Courtesy of Berkshire Athenaeum.*

residence in the mid-nineteenth century on a town street, how and when was it called a cottage? When the house was sold to William L. Joslin in 1874, it became the family's second home. They renovated and enlarged the house, the grounds were extended and voilà!—a Berkshire cottage.

Sometimes there was no difference between a Pittsfield millionaire's house and a cottage. Just as had Wirt Walker and Dr. Coolidge, Bishop George Worthington moved to Pittsfield for his health. Worthington purchased Henry W. Bishop's cottage and made it his primary house when Bishop built his second cottage, Wiaka. A cottage became a primary Pittsfield home of a respected citizen in the same way that the Sampson cottage became a primary Pittsfield home after the death of cottager E.P. Sampson.

In short, Pittsfield created its own millionaires capable of purchasing or building a home of equal heft and adornment as any Berkshire cottage. It made Pittsfield distinct from any other Gilded Age resort and prompted the question: How did they do it?

MONEY AND POWER: PITTSFIELD AND THE GILDED AGE

They came from Great Barrington, Dalton and South Lee, invited by clever and successful Pittsfield businessmen. In Pittsfield they founded three businesses that not only employed the largest number of workers, but also established Pittsfield as a forerunner in Gilded Age production. They were William Stanley, Arthur Eaton and W. Murray Crane.

THE STANLEY WORKS

He was tall, thin and twenty-one years old—brimming with ideas, in constant motion and, like the medium he would perfect, a live wire. His father wanted him to remain in school and become a lawyer, but after completing undergraduate studies at Yale, he wrote to his father: "I've had it." He was off to pursue his dream of inventing. His name was William Stanley; the year was 1879.

In December 1879 Thomas Alva Edison caused a filament in a glass globe to glow with light using electricity. It was lucky for all of us that the invention of the electric generator was very, very close to that of the Edison light bulb. Otherwise, we would still be lighting a candle or cursing the proverbial darkness. Edison was a devotee of direct current (DC), which could only transmit electricity over short distances. Stanley thought he had a better idea. Of course, at the time he was working as an electrician in a fire alarm company, but his opportunity was coming.

In 1881, Stanley impressed prolific inventor Hiram S. Maxim. Maxim took Stanley on as his assistant at the United States Electric Company. From that moment, Stanley's rise was rapid. He moved from U.S. Electric to Westinghouse Electric in Pittsburgh. He was certain that alternating current (AC) was the answer to providing energy for homes and businesses, but he had not proved it to Westinghouse. Stanley fell ill and returned to his family in Great Barrington to recuperate.

In March 1886 William Stanley performed a small experiment: he lit with electricity a few stores on Main Street in Great Barrington. It was the first practical application of his patented transformer that allowed the use of alternating rather than direct current. Stanley now needed a bigger canvas on which to paint his vision of the future. He wanted to demonstrate that with AC he could light the world; or if not the world, at least a broader geographic area and greater number of consumers.

Almost immediately, Pittsfield businessmen William W. Gamwell, W.A. Whittlesey and William R. Plunkett perceived the value of Stanley's experiment and invited him to move to Pittsfield. They offered to bankroll Stanley with an initial investment of $25,000. J.P. Morgan had only invested $30,000 in Edison. Stanley accepted.

By 1891, the Stanley Electric Manufacturing Company and Stanley Laboratories were the largest employers in Pittsfield. Locals referred to them simply as "the Stanley Works." John Kelly and C.C. Chesney, electrical engineers, joined Stanley in Pittsfield, and the three developed the SKC transformer and the SKC generator. By 1895, electricity was becoming essential to American industry and the American standard of living.

The *New York Times* wrote: "[Stanley] Motors furnish evidence that power can be transmitted hundreds of miles by two phase alternating currents over wires and drive any kind of machinery." What they were driving was more than machinery; they were driving the Gilded Age—the richest burst of economic growth in our history.

So it was that after 1892 the wars began. The story of the electric company wars can be told in a brief sentence: if as the number of consumers multiplied, the number of providers shrunk, profits would grow exponentially. Competition was brutal. The takeovers made present-day consolidations look like playground games. They were correctly called the "Patent Wars"—bloody and deadly to all but the largest companies. To survive, J.P. Morgan convinced Edison to merge with Thompson-Houston, thus forming General Electric (GE). GE

William Stanley as a young man. *Courtesy of the Berkshire Athenaeum.*

Stanley Home in Pittsfield. *Courtesy of the Berkshire Athenaeum.*

and Westinghouse filed more than six hundred patent and copyright infringement lawsuits against each other and everyone else. Finally Westinghouse and GE agreed that they were killing each other and signed a cross licensing agreement, giving each blanket permission to use the other's patents. That left William Stanley alone—the last man standing. The year was 1896. The Stanley Works were six years old and had flourished, showing a healthy profit. Still, in that business environment the principal investors, men of Pittsfield, believed it mandatory to increase capital stock from $300,000 to $500,000 to protect themselves.

It was long past the time when electricity was considered a magic trick. Experts marveled at the rapidity with which its use had grown. Across the country, the Stanley Works played a leading role in making electric power and machinery available. At home, the Stanley Works were Pittsfield's largest employers. The owners and major investors were local men; the capital was raised locally; and the managers were locals. These locals reinvested in their hometown. The value of the company to Pittsfield seemed a proven point and the security of its future was in the municipal interest. The major investors believed Pittsfield citizens would step up to protect the Stanley Works from a takeover by outside interests. All that was needed from ordinary citizens was the last $80,000. And yet...

Of the capital stock issued, $80,000 remained unsubscribed. It was shocking to the managers: for lack of $80,000—$2 per citizen of Pittsfield—the Stanley Works were vulnerable. The door was open for a competitor, and the Roebling Company was able to buy the controlling share. An outlander now controlled Pittsfield's largest employer. If they moved the plants, it would devastate Pittsfield.

As the century drew to a close, Stanley turned to inventions not associated with electricity. One result was the very popular Stanley vacuum bottle (the "thermos").

EATON PAPER

Arthur W. Eaton of the Hurlbut Paper Company in South Lee came to Pittsfield in 1892 with an idea to fill a niche in the market. Americans purchased fine writing paper from Europe, and Eaton was convinced that the production of fine writing paper in delicate colors with embossing and engraving equal to the writing paper produced abroad could be made in Pittsfield. Eaton purchased the Terry Clock Factory and convinced Hurlbut to expand. Eaton Hurlbut was opened for business, but too soon Hurlbut faltered financially. When the American Writing Paper Company purchased the Hurlbut manufactory, Eaton negotiated the purchase of Eaton Hurlbut, renaming it Eaton & Pike.

The Gilded Age was not a time of introspection. What you saw was the most important. Members of society read character and social position into garments, jewels and cottages—why not stationary?

To bolster the idea, and boost sales, Eaton commissioned a book on the art and etiquette of letter writing. An excerpt informs the potential purchaser of fine paper:

> *The delicate grey envelope and the wrought silver monogram may be as indicative of the charm of the correspondent as her fine writing and subtly expressed thoughts...the rugged character of another* [man] *may be complimented by his choice of strong large sheets with a simple block letter die.*[21]

Eaton was right about both the increasing number of literate Americans and their desire to express themselves well on fine paper. Soon his company, now the Eaton, Crane & Pike Company of Massachusetts, grew to one thousand employees, and it had to reach out to surrounding Berkshire communities for employees.

In 1915 the company was selected as a feature at the Panama-Pacific International Exposition in San Francisco, a national exhibition of American products. The Eaton, Crane & Pike booth drew large crowds, and deservedly, for it was a working exhibit demonstrating papermaking.

The models built for the exhibition were displayed at Tiffany & Co. on Fifth Avenue in New York City because Eaton, Crane & Pike was the only stationary Tiffany carried.

CRANE PAPER

The Crane Paper Company was established in Dalton in 1801. Crane could figure the payroll on the fingers of one hand—one engineer, one vat man, one coucher and a general helper. In the day when paper was still handmade, a coucher was the one who transferred the wet mat from the vat to absorbent felt so it could be pressed dry. It was certainly not a large company, but Crane had big ideas.

In the early 1800s, Zenas Crane placed an ad in the *Pittsfield Sun*: "Americans! Encourage your own manufactories and they will improve. Ladies, save your RAGS." In the staid Massachusetts town, Crane's further request raised eyebrows—ladies save your underwear and nighties. Until then, one did not mention a lady's undergarments or their tattered remains. Why ever did Mr. Crane mention them, and what did he mean to do with them? Crane was a papermaker and he had an idea for better paper. Often the undergarments were made of linen. Linen added to pulp in the manufacturing process created a stronger paper. By 1847 Crane paper was deemed very special because of the method in which the linen threads were cleverly incorporated lengthwise into the paper.

Eaton House. *Courtesy of the Berkshire Athenaeum.*

Eaton House. *Courtesy of the Berkshire Athenaeum.*

In 1879 when the Federal government was searching for a single provider of all the paper for United States currency, the Cranes were ready. Murray Crane traveled to Washington, D.C., to submit his proposal and paper samples. Competition was brutal and word got around that Crane paper was somehow different—maybe better. So, on May 27 when bids were due, a competitor locked Crane in his hotel room to prevent him from submitting his proposal. However, before air conditioning bedrooms had transoms—small windows over the door that could be lowered to allow air to flow into the rooms without opening the doors.

According to the story, Crane crawled up, over and out through the transom and submitted his bid on time.

Crane Paper Company secured its most illustrious customer—the United States government. Crane's crafty insertion of linen threads made Crane paper harder to counterfeit, and it felt more like money. From that day to this, all U.S. paper currency has been made in Berkshire County by Crane & Co. Wherever the buck might stop, it started in Berkshire County.

Washington D.C. July 21, 1886...Our bid accepted. Only one submitted. Contract will be made out soon—same price as last year. W.M. (Murray) Crane.[22]

When the contract with the government to manufacture the paper for America's money was renewed in 1886, a new mill was required. The old Thomas Colt mill stood deserted at the edge of the Pittsfield-Dalton town line. The Crane family bought and retooled it. They also built special artesian wells to supply the constant flow of pure water required to produce the special paper. Government Mill became one of Pittsfield's most successful industries, employing 55 people in 1865. By the 1880s, the Cranes had 5 paper mills operating in Pittsfield and Dalton with 500 employees. By 1901, total employment reached 950 people.

In April 1892 a fire broke out at Government Mill. It was after-hours and only the security guard, Martin Kelly, was on the property. He discovered the fire and sounded the alarm. Although no one was hurt, damage to the mill was estimated at $100,000. The mill was insured for only $40,000. Nevertheless, the Cranes immediately rebuilt. Production began again, and as every crate of paper left the mill, it was stamped and addressed to: "The Honorable Secretary of the Treasury Washington D.C."

Now the driving forces of the Gilded Age were all being manufactured in Pittsfield—electricity, paper money and fine paper for the upper class and the growing population of literate Americans. To a large degree America was shaped for the next century during the Gilded Age, and Pittsfield had a role in shaping the Gilded Age. It manufactured money and power; that is, the paper for currency and the power that would speed manufacturing and raise the standard of living—electricity. Pittsfield was central to the era if not at the center of the Gilded Age world.

So there it was—Pittsfield as it would be for the next century—a small city of great importance, its economy assured. Or was it? Too often history moves from war to war, only finding significance in cannon fire, the words of the powerful and the deeds of the exceptional. For Pittsfield, the moment that changed everything was quiet, done in the ordinary course of business, and the key players were its ordinary citizens. Nonetheless, it was a moment that changed what Pittsfield would be for the next one hundred years. When the citizens of Pittsfield failed to subscribe to $80,000 of outstanding shares in the Stanley Works and they were sold instead to an outside company, the die was cast. Roebling did not move the plants—it sold its Pittsfield holdings to General Electric. No other single event did more to shape Pittsfield during the twentieth century than the loss of local control of the Stanley Works in 1896. Pittsfield, after the Gilded Age, became a company town. That was later—for now, Pittsfield hummed.

ALL AROUND
THE TOWN

The Stanley Works, Eaton, Crane & Pike and Government Mill were key industries, but not the only ones in Pittsfield. During the Gilded Age, a slogan emerged: "Made in Berkshire." It was affixed to shoes and thread, trucks and automobiles, paper and stationery, electric generators, transformers, meters and machines. Pittsfield was called the "metropolis in the mountains" in an effort to communicate its many features. It was a manufacturing, trade and transportation center, as well as a clean and beautiful summer resort. In many other parts of America, those characteristics would constitute a contradiction in terms.

The convergence of all lines into Berkshire County was at Pittsfield. If a track helped a town grow, the convergence of all tracks was a bonanza. South Berkshire County hastened to lay track northward to connect to Pittsfield. Then the talk of electric trolley cars began.

During the Gilded Age, travel within the town changed radically. In 1885 travel on foot or horseback was common but could be challenging. There were no paved roads, few sidewalks and no crosswalks. Trolleys were horse drawn. Ladies complained that their dresses were ruined in one outing as the hems brushed in mud (and worse). Then in March, "The Horse Damage Case" against Pittsfield commenced.

A petition was signed by seven residents and read: "We the undersigned do affirm that the road leading from West Street to Stearnsville was on March 31, 1885 in no fit condition for any horse to travel upon." Appended to it was a bill for $117 as follows: "damage to horse $50.00, for services of Dr. Brackins $2.00, to keep care of horse 5 weeks $40.00, and hiring horse for twenty days $15.00." The two documents were submitted to the court, but there was no record of the town paying the damages. Whether Pittsfield did or not, it was the beginning of improved intracity transportation.

The Roosevelt carriage and the trolley race down South Street. *Courtesy of the Berkshire Athenaeum.*

In 1890 Pittsfield Street Railway with its horse-drawn cars was purchased by local businessmen and converted into the Pittsfield Electric Railway. In 1901, a consortium of county men (from Pittsfield, Dalton, Westfield and Great Barrington) formed the Berkshire Street Railway.

William C. Whitney, a Berkshire cottager, was heavily invested in the development of metropolitan trolley systems. In 1896 an important meeting was held in New York that influenced trolley lines throughout the country. Interviewed after the meeting,

Whitney said it was determined that while compressed air locomotion was trustworthy and stood up in all weather, as did electric trolley cars, "to lay a cable for compressed air trolleys cost $125,000 per mile and to prepare a street and put in an electric wire cost only $40,000 per mile." While Whitney denied that the compressed air system was being abandoned, and may be used where conditions dictated, it sounded the death knell for the one form of propulsion and the birth of the electric trolley system in American cities.

The trolley brought to the middle and working classes freedom of movement previously known only to the very rich. The cottagers and wealthy Pittsfield citizens eschewed the trolley. They had, as always, private transportation.

In October 1892 the *Century Magazine* wrote, "The public today takes such a lively interest in all matters appertaining to road-coaching that a few notes [about the sport] from the best authorities will be welcome." The "matters appertaining" had to do with the optimum road conditions and the best horses, coaches and driving style, as well as problems attendant upon stabling.

The road surface best suited for coaching was macadam made with volcanic rock—never sedimentary road. "It disintegrates and becomes 'wooly' in wet weather." The best road of all has a medium crown. Over such a surface, coaches can pass one another without tipping on uneven shoulders. Furthermore, a horse can maintain a speed of one mile per three minutes for a distance of almost nine miles when the surface is hard and gently banked. Finally, the road selected should be a place of beauty. The roadbed should be "pretty smooth as nothing is more disagreeable than being shaken up"; there should be a fine vista and good cuisine.

The coaching referred to was not simple transport from place to place; it was a race. It had pit stops and a change of horses. It had rules and required talented drivers. It was Le Mans in slow motion.

"Horsing" a coach was tricky. The best team was all of one type of horse, not an odd lot. The longer the race, the more likely that one would have to "horse a portion"; that is, change the team to suit the conditions of that portion of the road race. Selecting a team for a particular portion was related to strategy. The best strategy was to go ten miles per hour as often as possible. One achieved this overall speed by taking the "coach as rapidly as possible over all falling ground." Being instructed to go as fast as possible down hill seemed fairly obvious, but less intelligible were the commands: "Never put the horses in their bridles; avoid causing the horses to haul their pole chains, or bend their hocks."

Even trickier was the art of horse keeping and stabling. The 1892 article continued:

It is difficult to find men at reasonable wages who at the same time thoroughly understand four-horse work. In this respect the old coachman had the advantage. The present horse-keepers are, as a rule, difficult to manage, conceited, and love strong liquor.

The coach itself was a matter of great pride and importance. Different styles performed differently, and some superior to others. The key, though, seemed to be the number of riders: never more than six inside or seven outside. More than that number slowed the horses. The smart carriage with four horses and brass should endeavor to be quiet. The offending element was the coach horn. "Now that road coaching is on the increase in America, it is hoped that there will be a judicious and limited use of the horn."

The driving was, it seemed, left to the driver, and he should only be judged by his overall performance—if he wins, he drove well. Whether the reins should be buckled or hang loose, whether the whip and reins should be thrown down or carried down as the driver descends the box "are minor details that form food for many petty discussions not worth the acrimony they arouse."

It was a dangerous precedent for drivers to believe the end justified the means. On a fateful day in 1902, it was perhaps the presence on Pittsfield's South Street of a trolley and a private horse-drawn carriage that caused the problem. Witnesses said they were racing—testing the old mode of travel against the new.

It was Pittsfield Electric Railway Car 29, an eight-bench open car, on the "Country Club Line" that struck the rear wheel of an open landau, pitching the carriage passengers into South Street. It might have been an accident soon forgotten if the passengers had not been the president of the United States, the governor of Massachusetts, the president's secret service agent and the secretary of commerce.

On September 3, 1902, the first secret service agent was killed in the line of duty. William Craig, assigned to protect President Theodore Roosevelt, died just two hundred yards north of their destination, the Pittsfield Country Club. Governor W. Murray

Crane was unhurt; President Roosevelt and Secretary George B. Cortelyou suffered minor cuts and bruises. One of the four horses was so severely injured that it had to be put down. The reaction was highly charged and word spread across the country.

The motorman, Euclid Madden, and the conductor, James Kelly, were charged. Kelly was released, but Madden was fined $300 and served six months. The Pittsfield Electric Railway Company paid the fine for Madden and rehired him when he was released from the Berkshire County House of Corrections. It was an indication that many felt he had been made a scapegoat in a rush to appease the public outrage. There were no winners or losers that day, only survivors and casualties.

Early in the Gilded Age, the two novel forms of transportation were the automobile and the bicycle. The cottagers brought the "new-fangled machines" (bicycles) to The Berkshires. They were the first celebrities—their every move was recorded, their every fashion imitated and where the cottagers went others followed—and the public copied the mode of transport. Soon there were so many cyclists that they formed the Berkshire County Wheelman's Club in Pittsfield. One member, Isaac Sackett, possessed a popular model, Pope's high-type bicycle.

The high-type faded and was manufactured no more. Other bicycles and tricycles became children's toys. The reemergence of the bicycle for adults would come later.

The other cottager fad had a very different fate. At first the automobile was barely tolerated—they were noisy and scared the horses. Municipalities passed ordinances limiting the speed, routes and hours they could travel. The operators of the auto were also sorely challenged. Roads were not paved. Autos were open, windscreens were optional and without a top, a windscreen was ineffectual. Automobilists wore caps or hats, goggles and linen garments over their clothes that buttoned down the front from throat to ankles. They were called dusters—exactly the right name for the required garment drivers wore to protect clothes and skin as the dust from the road was kicked up and any manner of particles fell down upon them.

In 1904, Frank Wyland and Clarence Hollister, two employees of the Stanley Electric Company, incorporated the

Isaac Sackett on Pope high-type bicycle. *Courtesy of Christopher Baumann.*

The Berkshire automobile. *Courtesy of the Berkshire Athenaeum.*

Berkshire Automobile Company. By 1905, they produced their first automobile in their Pittsfield factory. The firm produced six different models of vehicles. "The Berkshire" performed competently in trial races and made the trip from Berkshire to Boston in less than six hours. That was very good time, and yet Berkshire Auto went out of business by 1912. That was not the experience of Henry Ford and other auto manufacturers.

By the turn of the century, trolleys ran on an electric wire, the ladies insisted on sidewalks and crosswalks and the increasing number of auto drivers demanded paved roads. There were only 144 miles of paved road in the United States and two of those miles (on five roads) were in Pittsfield. Gradually horse droppings, hitching posts and mud were replaced with the occasional spark from a trolley line, parking slots, oil slicks, gas fumes and car horns. Through the changes, in the distance, was heard the constancy of the train whistle.

The screech of the whistle—the clang and toot, the fumes and exhaust—heralded a new age. They freed the working class to accept work at a greater distance from home. They enhanced their quality of life by making parks, lakes and recreation areas accessible on their days off. They did not quite equal, but approximated, the mobility enjoyed by the upper classes. With ease, the middle class could find their way to the shopping streets of Pittsfield from any village in the county. The beneficiaries of public transportation were the people and the city. As a result, Pittsfield business and industry had manpower; Pittsfield commerce had a larger pool of customers with buying power; and Pittsfield boomed.

THEY GOT IT ALL
IN PITTSFIELD

Pittsfield seemed to have it all—the glamour of the cottagers, prosperous industrial and commercial centers and the beauty of the Berkshire Hills. What Pittsfield lacked to be a full-fledged Gilded Age resort was a resort hotel. In 1887 a scion of the Red Lion Inn in Stockbridge saved the day and solved Pittsfield's problem so they could truly say: "They got it all in Pittsfield."

Arthur W. Plumb was the son of Henry and nephew of Charles Plumb, owner/managers of the Red Lion Inn. His cousin was Heaton Treadway, builder of Heaton Hall, another Stockbridge hotel. Arthur Plumb started his hotel career as a bellboy at the Red Lion Inn. He worked his way up to clerk and learned the business well. As he looked over the abandoned and crumbling buildings of the former Maplewood Young Ladies Institute, he saw a first-class resort hotel—an idea that was no less than his birthright.

Plumb leased the Maplewood buildings in 1887 and purchased the property in 1889. He transformed the Maplewood into a resort hotel. Just as Plumb learned his trade as a Red Lion Inn hotel clerk and applied the lessons at the Maplewood, Allen T. Treadway, future owner of the Red Lion, joined the staff as a clerk at the Maplewood.

Hotel clerk at the Maplewood was an important job as they welcomed presidents and peers of the realm, stars of the theatrical stage and some of the most illustrious guests of the business world. *Berkshire Resort Topics* reported that Mr. and Mrs. George Pullman, Mr. William G. and Mr. W.A. Rockefeller, Mr. and Mrs. Henry Ford and H.M. Phelps Stokes—the magnates of the palace railway car, Standard Oil, the automobile and real estate—were "At the Maplewood."

Having it all included entertainment and recreation. As the population grew and more land was used for housing, Pittsfield wisely set aside land for parks. In the city limits there were lakes and unspoiled wilderness, manicured parks and picnic areas,

The Maplewood. *Courtesy of the Berkshire Athenaeum.*

boating, skating and bicycling. In 1892 Pittsfield built one of the first baseball fields, Waconah Park.

The trolley lines encouraged intracounty travel by creating recreation areas as destination points. Berkshire Park, a 110-acre trolley park, was established in 1902. It had a dance pavilion, vaudeville theater, restaurant, picnic area, small lake, skating rink, burro rides, observation tower and most popular of all, the first permanent carousel in Pittsfield. Inadvertently, these parks served a conservation purpose because in booming Pittsfield, hundreds of acres were preserved from home or factory building.

In center city, theaters prospered. Those seeking diversion could find it from South Street to North Street, at the Colonial, Academy of Music, Music Hall and later, motion picture theaters.

When Cebra Quackenbush dedicated his theater, the Academy of Music, on December 16, 1872, it was indeed a source of civic pride and high hopes. It was reported that, "Quackenbush has added significantly to the advantages of the town."[23]

Quackenbush hired the Boston architect, Louis Weissbein, who designed the Pittsfield jail, the county courthouse and the Berkshire Life Building. The result was a three-story brick building located on North Street. The seating capacity was twelve hundred. It had steam heat and gas lighting.

A clerk stands at the desk in the lobby of the Wendell Hotel. *Courtesy of the Berkshire Athenaeum.*

The academy opened with a production of *Leah, the Forsaken*. In the next nineteen years at the academy, audiences were treated to everything from animal acts to opera. A broadside for the 1885 production of *Ten Nights in a Bar Room* enthuses: "A correct picture of intemperance…sobs and tears from auditors of both sexes…a play that has everywhere proven a sensation unparalleled in the history of drama." Step aside, Shakespeare; make way for T.S. Arthur and his temperance drama in five acts.

Quackenbush was what they used to call a "warm" man—not crooked, certainly, just "too clever by half" and "pushing" with a sharp eye for the main chance. Those combined characteristics, however, resulted in quite a triumph for Pittsfield. Quackenbush's greatest theatrical coup took place not inside, but outside of the theater in the middle of North Street.

William Cody was a true cowboy. He was awarded the Congressional Medal of Honor in 1872 for his service in the

Academy of Music. *Courtesy of the Berkshire Athenaeum.*

United States Army in the West. Ned Buntline (pen name of the writer E.Z.C. Judson) transformed the real-life cowboy into an American myth. Beginning in 1869, Buntline mixed fact and fiction in his dime novels to create "Buffalo Bill." At Buntline's urging, Cody agreed to play a cowboy onstage. Enter Cebra Quackenbush.

Quackenbush furnished the capital for "Buffalo Bill" Cody and "Wild Bill" Hickok to appear in Pittsfield. His idea was not that they act in a play but rather that they create their own show—part demonstration, part circus. It was the first performance of what would become *Buffalo Bill's Wild West Show*, and that first performance was in Pittsfield.

The show was a great success, and the outdoor extravaganza grew to dramatize a buffalo hunt, a Native American attack and a Pony Express ride. In later years *Buffalo Bill's Wild West Show* starred Annie Oakley and for one season, Sitting Bull. Cody created an act that toured the country for three decades, earned an international reputation and was the genesis of an enduring image of the American West. To the end of his days, Cody credited Quackenbush with starting his career.

Neither *Buffalo Bill* nor *Ten Days in a Bar Room* was Quackenbush's only contribution to Pittsfield. In building the Academy of Music, Quackenbush created the largest space available for social gatherings in the town; therefore, the academy was the site of many historical Pittsfield events. In 1877, a crowd of three hundred gathered at the academy to watch the first local demonstration of the telephone. In 1891, it was the scene of celebration for the dissolution of the Pittsfield town government and inauguration of Pittsfield as a city.

The construction of the theater was at once its greatest asset and its downfall. The theater was on the second and third floors with shops on the street level. Quackenbush wanted the shops to bring in additional income to underwrite the theatrical productions. Unfortunately, the climb to the second floor for performances around a single narrow stairway created a traffic jam that displeased patrons and struck fear into the hearts of city officials. What would happen if fire broke out? Visions of over twelve hundred people trapped on the upper floor of a burning building haunted city officials, and in 1891, the theater's license was suspended. The final production was shown on December 12, 1891, almost nineteen years to the day after the opening.

Eight years later the academy reopened under new management. The interior was redesigned. Seating was reduced to eleven hundred to allow for two staircases, and the stage was now eighty feet wide and thirty-seven feet deep and boasted thirty-five complete sets of scenery, two separate curtains and two rows of footlights. Electric lights replaced gas. Again, hopes for the benefit to the city ran high.

In 1897, in a special edition of the *Berkshire Evening Eagle*, a reporter wrote:

> *Probably no other class of people does more to advertise a city than what are commonly termed "show people." Give them full houses and they go away uttering encomiums* [odes] *of the strongest kind as to the enterprise of the people and* [the superiority of] *the town. Give the people only the best attractions so that a patron can rely that he will pass an enjoyable evening and they will react heartily by giving packed houses to every attraction.*

THE MERCHANTS OF PITTSFIELD

Commerce in Pittsfield burgeoned because industry created jobs. Jobs created a growing and concentrated population. Salaries created discretionary income for goods. Pittsfield merchants flourished. Completing the circle, many of the goods they sold were manufactured in Pittsfield—shoes, thread, stationary, glass, ink and, not to be overlooked, magic oil. Furthermore, Pittsfield commerce grew as a function of location. Pittsfield may not have been the exact physical center of Berkshire County, but it was close enough for Berkshire villagers to come to Pittsfield for goods and entertainment. Trains, trucks and trolleys traveled the county from end to end and allowed customers easy access. There was a Berkshire mantra: if a local was asked where to find anything from a nail to a needle, the answer was always, "You can get it in Pittsfield."

There was room for all kinds of products, including those of Jarvis Renne. Renne had a line of products: Renne's Magic Oil that "works like a charm," Renne's Magic Pain Killing Oil and Devine's Lozenges. Perhaps the last was a move from simple magic to "divine intervention." Make fun as we might, the business was successful from 1869 to 1879. In 1869, Jarvis Renne was listed as a peddler of magic oil. Son William joined the firm as manufacturer, and in 1876, the business was listed as William Renne & Sons.

While we do not have his recipe for magic oil, we can be fairly certain it did not make anyone violently ill or kill anyone outright. The reason is simple—no Renne left town under the cover of night. On the contrary, house and factory stood at 22 Frances Avenue for ten years, clearly marked with a large sign. After 1879, William remained at 22 Frances until his death in 1904 with no occupation listed. It would seem that ten years of labor paid for twenty-five years of retirement—and that was magic!

We do have the recipe for "Maxim's Lightning Cure—Good for what ails you." It was an unfortunate mixture of kerosene, camphor and herbs. Alden Knowles and Hudson Maxim were

Knowles and Maxim in the same suit. *Courtesy of the Berkshire Athenaeum.*

friends from their school days in Maine. They joined forces to make their fortune and failed spectacularly. They tramped across the country passing themselves off as phrenologists, faith healers and producers of their potent elixir. Finally, convinced that healing was not his métier, Maxim turned to what was, in fact, the family business—inventing.

Knowles and Maxim found success in Pittsfield as ink manufacturers and publishers when Maxim invented a formula for ink and combined that with Knowles's talent for illustration. The result was the Knowles and Maxim store, the Real Penwork Company on North Street that sold ink and nibs, and their book, *The Real Penwork: Self-Instruction in Penmanship.*

As Eaton would do, Knowles and Maxim wrote a book demonstrating fine penmanship and providing stencils to create decorations for invitations and special notes. Naturally, the instructions were easier to follow if the penman used Knowles and Maxim pens and nibs, and would be more

Jennie Maxim with her nine-week-old son. *Courtesy of the Berkshire Athenaeum.*

beautiful with Knowles and Maxim colored inks. As the book was ready for publication, they knew they had to dress for success; unfortunately, they could afford only one business suit. The photograph required for the front of *The Real Penwork* shows both aspiring merchants wearing the same suit. The photographer took a photograph of one partner in the suit, waited while Knowles and Maxim changed clothes, and then photographed the other partner. It was time-lapse photography nineteenth-century style. The ploy worked. The book and their business were a success.

As Maxim settled into the life of the merchant class in Pittsfield, he met and married a Pittsfield farmer's daughter and schoolteacher, Miss Jane (Jennie) Morrow. Together they had a son, and shortly thereafter, Maxim deserted wife and child. He literally went "off to see the King," or more accurately the Prince of Wales. Hudson Maxim followed the invention of superior ink with an invention of smokeless explosive powder and then a Maxim bullet. Maxim accepted an invitation to England where the Prince of Wales endorsed (by firing) the Maxim bullet. In the beginning he wrote home, promising to return—someday: "Kent England July 11, 1888 My darling...will have to wait here a little longer before I know anything for certain one way or another."

After stringing his poor wife along for months, Maxim did return to the United States, but not to hearth and home—not to Pittsfield. He settled in New Jersey and set to work on a series of inventions relating to explosives and torpedoes. The Dupont Company purchased the patents, and Maxim became a wealthy and famous man.

By 1893, Jane Morrow Maxim resigned to the fact of desertion and did two things: she divorced Maxim, and in the backroom of the Real Penwork Company, she set up the Union for Home Work. The union was a Pittsfield charity to aid other women in similar circumstances. Jennie continued to run the business her husband had left behind until the typewriter put pen and ink out of business.

When that business failed, she moved to South Street and opened an antique business. She wrote a newspaper column and raised her son alone. She was a strong and successful woman in an age when many women were idle and dependent. She was aided by Pittsfield itself—it was a community that supported women in the "masculine" roles of businesswoman, writer and founder of a charitable organization.

Edward A. Larkin, a journeyman tailor, arrived in Pittsfield during the "Storm of '88." It was March 11, 1888, and the storm dumped forty to fifty inches of snow. When the nor'easter set in, drifts were reported as high as thirty-five feet. Larkin could barely make it from Union Station to the Burbank Hotel just across the street.

Entering the lobby, his luck changed. Decades before, Mr. Burbank came into Pittsfield with empty pockets. By 1888,

The Burbank Hotel across from Union Station. *Courtesy of the Berkshire Athenaeum.*

he was an established and wealthy Pittsfield citizen with hotels and real estate, but Burbank never forgot his roots. He welcomed Mr. Larkin, and invited him to stay for free. During his stay, Larkin met other local men marooned at the hotel. It was the start of a tailoring business that lasted until his death.

Over three decades, he liked to say, "I made a boy's first long pants, and the suit they laid him out in." Larkin bridged the gap between upstairs and down. He made clothes for the wealthy and uniforms for their servants. Edward A. Larkin, tailor—later, owner of Larkin's retail store—was a fixture on North Street from 1890 to 1961. And the famous Knowles-Maxim suit, was it a Larkin original? Possibly.

The absence of television and radio during the Gilded Age did not spell relief from commercial advertising. It only meant ads came in a different form. The merchants created trade cards, and they were ubiquitous. Trade cards advertised goods manufactured in Pittsfield and Pittsfield businesses: "Pittsfield Coal: It's hot stuff." They also advertised the town of Pittsfield itself: "From a needle to a nail, they got everything in Pittsfield." My favorite read: "Come to Pittsfield and see what happens." It had a picture of a man and woman kissing in a hot air balloon. Ah, the link between sex and advertising was forged long before our modern age.

WHITE COLLAR AND BLUE

The difference between a white collar and a collarless shirt, a suit and a uniform told a powerful tale of economic class and profession. Perhaps because subtlety was prized over clarity in verbal communication, many objects were invested with symbolic meaning. Chief among these wordless messengers were the clothes on your back. In the Gilded Age, one could determine the class of a person as they approached.

All blue-collar workers had uniforms, whether that of a footmen or train conductor, a cook, housemaid or nurse. The dress a milady wore cost more than the annual wages of the footman who opened the door for her. Middle-class ladies tried their best to imitate the cottagers, but appreciated the dresses found at Kennedy & MacInnes. Their dresses were attractive and well made, but they were also practical. When worn they appeared to be dresses but were actually two-piece outfits. One skirt had two matching tops. For one price, the woman had alternate tops for day and evening wear. The classes dressed differently, lived differently and ate differently.

In 1907 John T. McLaughlin opened the Bridge Lunch. A diner popular with workers, it was said fourteen hundred people lunched there daily although there were only eighteen stools. Either the statistics were wrong or workers waited a long time to eat.

In a blue-collar household there might be an all-work table in a single living room. In a middle-class household there were at least three rooms on the ground floor for dining, welcoming guests and retiring to an office or library.

On June 16, 1904, Henry M. Seaver, a Pittsfield architect, married Alice Wentworth. Miss Wentworth was the daughter of Dr. Walter Wentworth, a Stockbridge native who was educated as a physician in New York City and then returned to The Berkshires, where he established his practice in Pittsfield. He was a successful and revered doctor until his death in 1910. As an architect, Seaver helped transform the city. He was the architect

The exterior of the Henry Seaver House. *Courtesy of the Berkshire Athenaeum.*

of the Coolidge cottage Upwey, and after the turn of the century he designed the Berkshire Museum. The Berkshire Museum and the Colonial Theater were the twin centerpieces of new South Street. The Seavers were solid white-collar middle class, and their home reflected it. It was not the equivalent in size or adornment to Upwey, but it was more than adequate.

In the cottages, there were separate rooms for every imagined activity—a billiard room, library, dining room, salon, ballroom and music room.

The great houses were actually two residences in one—exclusive but mutually dependent. The servants' quarters and the workrooms were above and below, connected by narrow back stairs. A former maid at The Mount returned when the house was for sale just to walk down the main staircase, as she had never in all her years of service used the main, or family, stairs.

In 1882, an article about the "Legal Relations of Mistress and Servant" appeared in the *Century*. The article dealt only with "what remedy (the mistress) has for simple idleness and neglect of

The interior of Henry Seaver House. *Courtesy of the Berkshire Historical Society.*

duty." The remedy, of course, was dismissal and a bad character. Suits brought by servants were unimagined. Slandering a servant by writing an undeserved bad character was not possible, as characters were legally privileged communications between employers. The idea that the servant had rights, beyond payment for time served, was not considered.

The hours were long, but the surroundings were grand. The labor was constant but not as onerous as working in the mines. The trick was that owners did not want to see the work being done; therefore, much had to be done before the family rose in the morning. In every cottage, there were narrow doors and narrow stairs—back hallways—for staff to slip down and out of sight when the family and their friends were using the main rooms. The most beloved cottagers were those who kept to a routine so the staff knew when they would be where and could literally work around them. If caught trimming a hedge by cottagers out for a stroll in their grounds, gardeners dived out of sight and lay face down in the dirt until the lady of the house passed.

In the late 1880s, Mrs. Schuyler Van Rensselaer, a writer of social commentary, complained that young girls who preferred factory work or hospital work to a domestic position were foolish and putting their virtue at risk. After all, a domestic servant was given food and shelter in the safety of a gentleman's home. In 1889 she wrote, "Our servants are better paid than any other women and sheltered from many of the temptations that surround working girls." She found it incomprehensible that a girl would choose any other work.

Seemingly in answer to Mrs. Van Rensselaer's concern, Pittsfield businesses provided boardinghouses for their female employees. Eaton, Crane & Pike offered "first-class board" with supervision for "out of town girls—16 and older" who wished to move to Pittsfield and work in the factory.

For a young Pittsfield girl who had to make a living wage, the choices were limited. For the ever-growing female workforce there was domestic work, increasingly in Pittsfield there was factory work and finally, there was nursing. Although respected as a profession today, and demanding training then as now, nursing was still looked upon as not necessarily superior to domestic work. When Henry W. Bishop established a nursing school in memory of his son, secure housing for the nurses-in-training was provided. At the end of the Gilded Age, as the cottages were sold and abandoned, the William Russell Allen House was used first as a laying-in hospital, and later as housing for the nurses.

The cottagers may have earned as much as $1,000 to $10,000 per day, while laborers earned as little as $1 a day and supervisors earned about $250 to $500 per week. White-collar professions earned more, but none collected a salary near the daily income of the Gilded Age economic elite. As the Gilded Age drew to a close, wages had increased, but not by much. Ledgers from the Wendell Hotel show weekly salaries as follows:

Chef: $39/week
Pot washer: $11/week
Office girl/telephone girl: $12/week
Housekeepers: $8/week

Socioeconomic hierarchy was not only a fact between the classes; there was also a hierarchy within the ranks of blue-collar workers. Whether they were in the hotel, the household or on the railroad or trolley lines, the supervisory positions earned two or three times more than the laborers working under them.

On June 2, 1909, there was a strike against the Pittsfield Electric Railway by the conductors. They formed into a union to make a joint petition. Paid a maximum of twenty-two and a half cents per hour, they demanded both more and less. They felt "first-year men" should be satisfied with twenty-one cents per hour, but men who had worked the line five years and longer should earn twenty-five cents (equivalent to $5 today). The strike was over almost before it began. The company granted the wage scale, provided they would disband the union. On June 3, the conductors returned to work.

The classes lived differently, dressed differently and ate differently. During the Gilded Age, the popular love stories were Cinderella stories wherein the girl finds love and a step-up in class—from scullery to palace. Cinderella stories were not limited to use by fiction writers; advertisers used them as well. The trade card "Come to Pittsfield and See what Happens" implied a young girl would find not just a job but also love. Was there any truth in advertising?

In 1866 William H.H. Clark, a returning Civil War veteran, took a job as switchman for the old Western Railway (later the Boston & Albany line). He lived with his family on Jubilee Hill and walked the line, lantern in hand.

Clark valued education and meant to make something more of himself. He returned to college to take commercial courses. It allowed him to expand his duties at the local rail yards from track maintenance to billing clerk of the line, bookkeeper of the freight charges, ticket seller and conductor on a branch line.

His daughter, Daisy May Clark, was born on Jubilee Hill in 1874. She grew up overlooking the railroad that employed her father and dreaming of life in the great houses. She was introduced to Erwin Stanley, a Yale graduate who came to Pittsfield to work as an electrical engineer for General Electric.

Francis houses and Renne's "Magic Oil" building on Jubilee Hill.

The roundhouse, hub of train travel. *Above,* Frances Avenue on Jubilee Hill; *above left,* the home of Renne's Magic Oil; *above right,* the home of William H.H. Clark. *Courtesy of Berkshire Scenic Railway.*

Love bloomed. The little girl from Jubilee Hill was wed, and Daisy moved from daughter of a blue-collar worker to wife of a white-collar professional surrounded by the trappings of a rising middle class. She honeymooned in Europe, returned to have her "at home" cards printed and lived in the gracious house of her dreams.

In 1891 the *Sunday Morning Call* ran a front-page article about love and marriage among the literati. "Perhaps the prettiest little romance of all is the story of how Rose Terry Cooke (of Pittsfield) won her husband."

Rose Terry may not be a household name today, but in the nineteenth century she was a well-respected and popular writer of short stories. Middle-aged, she had long since accepted that her brush with romance would be only in the pages of her stories and the lines of her poems. Little did she know that another was reading her work and admiring from afar.

Rollin H. Cooke was a humble bank cashier, but as luck would have it, he was the cashier at Rose's bank. He was significantly her junior, but he was not deterred. He approached her and bestowed upon her "gentleness, chivalry, and admiration." He won her over. They married and moved to Pittsfield, where they prospered. She continued to write the stories he admired while he rose to bank president and president of the Pittsfield Board of Trade. In this case it was the gentleman who stepped up in class through marriage. As president of the Pittsfield Board of Trade, perhaps he designed the trade card: "Come to Pittsfield and see what happens."

PART III

POLISHING THE GEM

THE REPOSITORIES

It has been said that history lights our steps to the future and informs our best decisions. If true, then Pittsfield would benefit from knowing its history from incorporation as a town to inauguration as a city, from Revolutionary War to Civil War to, of course, the Gilded Age.

The Gilded Age in Pittsfield was not just an unexamined part of both Pittsfield and Gilded Age history; it was a forgotten part. Pittsfield's history seemed to be told in fits and starts. Two hundred and forty years in three vignettes: Thomas Allen, the "Fighting Parson," bounded out of town to do battle at Ticonderoga and Bennington during the Revolutionary War; trains chugged into town prior to the Civil War; General Electric arrived in 1903. Fast-forward to today, and the end of the history lesson. Filling in the blanks could lead to surprise, delight and civic pride.

The "Fighting Parson" struggling at home to build the ministry lot to leave to his son; the son presiding over the fall until there was nothing left; the grandson arriving, triumphant, and reclaiming the Allen property parcel by parcel; the grandson extending the holdings; and then the modern age, just one Allen house left standing. The expanding and contracting as the story is told is like an accordion opening and closing; like the breathing of a living city.

A train arriving in 1846 and Henry Wadsworth Longfellow alighting; Longfellow come "a' courtin'," standing in the Nathan Appleton house awaiting his Fanny, seeing the clock on the stair; inspired, writing one of his best-known poems. The wrecker's ball, the house gone and with it the opportunity to stand where he stood, see what he saw, be inspired as he was inspired.

Pittsfield architects Joseph McArthur Vance and Henry Seaver perusing the clapboard houses and the tree-lined street typical of a New England town; designing the exteriors of a new city's cultural center; a theater architect, William McElfatrick, famous for designing the (first) Metropolitan Opera House and 266 other theaters, designing an interior; and then the houses are gone, and the Berkshire Museum and Colonial Theater rise up. The great Union Station built by Thomas Allen out of compromise promising prosperity for the town and comfort for the traveler, replaced by a white marble wonder—and then it too is gone. For a living, breathing city, change is inevitable.

Historians know how much Pittsfield has lost—the train station, England Brothers, the Thomas Allen houses, the Peace Party house, Abby Lodge and more. It is just that historians also know where you can still find them. In word and picture, the architectural treasures of Pittsfield still exist. In story and artifact, Pittsfield's history comes alive once more. This treasure trove is invulnerable to the wrecker's ball; it is safeguarded, and the way through is led by inestimable guides—all four Pittsfield train stations, Melville's desk and the pen with which he wrote, Stanley's blueprints, Oliver Wendell Holmes's library and Jennie Morrow Maxim's trademarks. They are professional storytellers, as historians always are, and they are standing their post at the local history room of the Berkshire Athenaeum and the Berkshire Historical Society in Pittsfield. They are the best friends of writers and scholars, teachers and history buffs—and could be the friends of economic developers and city planners. Our libraries and historical societies are our cache, but the repositories of our memories are the buildings. Many are gone, but one can mine for the gold, find the treasure underfoot and around the corner and be amazed on the streets of Pittsfield at how much historic architecture still exists.

Through buildings, we remember the details of our individual lives, and they tell the story of our collective life. When a building is torn down, a memory and a link to the past are torn out of the communal fabric.

Any municipality gains more by restoring extant buildings rather than by tearing down and building new. Contrary to prevailing wisdom, new buildings are not the cornerstones of economic growth. Building new creates no more construction

Allen House today, servant's stair. *Courtesy of William Russell Allen House Inc.*

"Moorish Room" as it appears today. *Courtesy of William Russell Allen House Inc.*

jobs than restoring. The number of jobs created once a business moves in is not a function of the mode of construction; materials available today do not compare in price and quality to the materials available 50, 100 or even 150 years ago. In the last century we have exhausted the supplies of many different woods, not to mention the skills in erecting and finishing that are no longer available. Building new condemns other parts of a city to wither and die while restoration revitalizes the neighborhoods most in need. Perhaps most importantly, a community should save its buildings because they are where the memories are stored.

Ask this of all the doubting Thomas's and proponents of "new is better": Haven't you taken a loved one to the "old neighborhood," pointed and started the story of your life with the words, "Look, that is the building where I first..." We all have.

Historians delight in oral histories. They add spice to the dish. Whether by using photographs or embarking on mini

Allen House today, front door. *Courtesy of William Russell Allen House Inc.*

field trips, the memories of the interviewees are enlivened by the sight of old buildings. The stories are often punctuated with the words, "I haven't thought of that in years. But now that I see that old building I remember."

Two octogenarians shared that experience. The buildings were on the streets of Pittsfield and the stories were full of love for a Pittsfield that once was. The subject was Saturday in Pittsfield.

She and her mother took the 12:20 train from Stockbridge and arrived in Pittsfield at 1:00 p.m. They ate wherever the budget allowed. If they were feeling wealthy, they went to the Berkshire Restaurant on West Street for the three-dollar meal. If they had only a moderate budget, they could have a nice midday supper at the Hub (near Bagel II) or the Rosa. When there was not much money at all, they sat at the counter at Newberry's and had a hot turkey sandwich.

"The turkey was paper thin—you could see right through it—but it was tasty."

Other times her mother would put up a supper, and they would supplement it with cakes at Joanne's Bakery or a chocolate frost at the soda fountain of the Professional Drugstore.

"That never hurt your budget. The frost was only fifteen cents."

He remembers the Berkshire, but preferred the Italian restaurant across the street called Busy Bee.

I tell you, you couldn't eat for laughing. I'd be sitting at the bar and hear a whooshing noise, look up, and there was your plate of food sliding down the bar. The bartender would ask, "want a roll?" and if you said yes, one would come at you lobbed over everyone's head like a soft pitch. It was something.

After the meal, mother and daughter would "shop North Street" for hats or dresses or textiles.

You could get anything on North Street at England Brothers and Wallace's. My favorite was Holden & Stone because if you bought something, they would put the money in a carriage that ran along a track. I loved to watch it go up and all over the store.

He remembers:

Locals went "up street" on Thursday nights to shop. Everyone loved that contraption at Holden and Stone. There was a metal track, and I think it was a mouse clamped onto the track. The whole thing worked on a pulley system to take the money from the sales floor to the second floor office, but first it went all over the place for fun. The best part was when they first put the money in and started the pulley, it took off real fast.

Then the ladies were off to the picture show at the Palace or the Capitol. "There were seven theaters in Pittsfield, seven! When we were kids we insisted upon going to the Palace because it had vaudeville." The Capitol (the Senior Center today) and the Union Square (Barrington Stage today) had first-run movies. "I remember the Capitol had upholstered armchairs that you could sit in for an extra charge. We never did." The Strand (on West) and the Cameo (on East) had

The interior of the restored Colonial Theater. *Courtesy of the Colonial Theater.*

second-run movies. Then there was the Tyler Theater in Morningside, and the seventh theater, of course, was the Colonial. "That is where I saw my first play, *Rip Van Winkle*." The movies started at 1:00 p.m. and showed continuously until 11:00 p.m.

She was in love with Nelson Eddy: "If it was a Nelson Eddy, I could sit through three times. I could follow a movie I loved around the county seeing it at the Mahaiwe, the Capitol and then at the second-run theaters."

The last bus to Stockbridge left at 11:00 p.m. At 10:30 p.m. mother and daughter walked along North Street to Park Square to catch the bus. The bus took sixty minutes compared to the twenty-minute train ride because "it wound all around" through Lenox, over to Lee and finally Stockbridge.

"Nice memories. I wish kids today could have a Saturday like that in Pittsfield complete with a fifteen cent chocolate frost."

The stories are not complete without both telling where the buildings were and whether they still stand. Regardless of the

Interior detail of the Colonial Theater. *Courtesy of the Colonial Theater.*

current use, if the building still stands they cite it as a small victory, as if the building itself held not just the memory, but also the hope that "those wonderful Saturdays in Pittsfield" will return someday.

PITTSFIELD'S SECOND GILDED AGE

When General Electric arrived in Pittsfield in 1903, the Stanley Works had one thousand employees, and the town had thirty-nine thousand citizens. GE-Pittsfield grew to thirteen thousand employees and the town population to fifty thousand. Pittsfield was a company town. In the company town there was cross dependence, mutual growth, shared goals and shared memory. The time before the marriage of town and company was forgotten, and when the company left—today GE employs less than seven hundred people in Pittsfield—there was a gasp, a loll. It was a period of mourning and depression. That passed, and today there is a burst of energy, revitalization—and a second Pittsfield Gilded Age?

On another day, a woman sits on her front porch. Over for a cup of tea, she enthuses, "I love Pittsfield. It's great, and it's coming back." Far from discouraged over what buildings are lost, she is versed in what historic buildings still stand and rejoices in their current uses. From her porch on her quiet street, shaded and redolent of overhanging trees in bloom, she names her favorites. The buildings span more than one hundred years in age, yet are still in use, still useful and still tell the stories of their time.

CAMPBELL'S COFFEE HOUSE AND THE MARTIN BLOCK

Two hundred years ago, in 1805, travel from Pittsfield was by horse, carriage or coach. From Pittsfield, west to Albany, south to Connecticut, north to Vermont or east to Boston, travel was facilitated by conveniently laid out and named roads: North Street, South Street, East and West Streets.

At the crossroad of these four arteries was the town square. Travel was slow, bumpy and sometimes dangerous. Places along the way to eat, rest and refresh the horses were essential. Campbell's Coffee House offered a hearty table, an ample bar and good conversation. Amid the crockery, over a mug of flip (beer, spirits and sugar heated with a hot iron), patrons argued about the Federalists versus the Democrats. Local businessmen discussed the founding of the Berkshire Agricultural Society (one of Pittsfield's first banks), the purchase of the town's first fire engine and the founding of some of the first Pittsfield manufactories.

In 1841, the glory days behind, Campbell sold the coffeehouse to Calvin Martin, a local attorney and his son-in-law. In 1850 Martin built the Martin Block on the site of the coffeehouse, but he did not tear Campbell's down. It was carefully moved to the corner of South and Broad where it served as an inn for another forty years. "Waste not, want not" were words Yankees lived by—buildings were rarely demolished.

Campbell was a well-respected businessman of Pittsfield, but in the end, his cleverest business investment in the future prosperity of Pittsfield was his family. His wife was the former Lucy Laflin, and when her sister Caroline Laflin married Zenas Marshall Crane, it brought all that paper cleverly improved with linen thread into the Campbell family circle. Caroline's son was Winthrop Murray Crane, who climbed over the transom to bring the contract for the United States currency to Pittsfield. One daughter married Calvin Martin, and the other two married manufacturers Ezekiel Colt and Thaddeus Clapp.

Today Pittsfield people can still eat in the Martin Block. Two hundred and one years of dining out at the same spot in Pittsfield. It is now called Patrick's Pub on Park Square.

THE BERKSHIRE LIFE BUILDING

When it opened in 1868, they called it "a superb building" and "the center of Pittsfield if not all of Berkshire County." It stood five stories high when the last addition was added. Inside were banks and an insurance company, the post office and a telegraph company, as well as two newspapers—the *Pittsfield Sun* and *Pittsfield Evening Eagle*. (Phinehas Allen moved his *Sun* to the building after the fire.) Upstairs there were doctors' offices and a banqueting hall. The hall was fifty-nine feet long and thirty feet wide. You could only dine there if you were a member of the Park Club or the Mason's or a member's invited guest. Dining there was more than a culinary experience; it was a social coup.

Under the heading of "the more things change the more they remain the same," Brix Wine Bar is still a gathering place to see and be seen. For 138 years, friends have gone to the Berkshire Life building at the corner of North and West Streets for a meal.

THE BURNS BLOCK

In 1883, grocer James Burns and his partner, brother David, bought property on North Street. They intended to erect a commercial building, but Mrs. Murray's house stood in the way. They did not tear down houses in those days. The Burns brothers moved Mrs. Murray's house to Union Street where she lived out her days in contentment. Business was good in their new building, and the Burns Block expanded. James tried the grocery business, the home furnishing business and banking. Like Campbell, his greatest contribution to Pittsfield's future was his family.

William Burns, James's son, attended Pittsfield High School, Williams College and Harvard Law School. He returned to Pittsfield and was named a justice of the Massachusetts Superior Court. Much respected and loved, on the day of his funeral, the Pittsfield Courthouse was closed; all members of the bar met on the steps and attended the funeral together.

Today you can still shop at the Burns Block on North Street, and when weary, stop in at the Spice Restaurant. Around the corner on Union Street, Mrs. Murray's house is finally gone, but in its place is the Union Theater, built in 1912. It was dedicated to that great man of the theater, Cebra Quackenbush. You can still attend a performance there today; it is now the Barrington Stage Theater.

THE BURBANK BUILDING

Abraham Burbank built this building in the 1870s, next door to the Boston and Albany engine house near Union Station. It was a warehouse. It served as a warehouse for many Pittsfield businesses, including the England Brothers. In the mid-twentieth century, however, the second floor became the meeting place for a men's club—the Monday Club. It was a club for dining and erudition. Members had two obligations: to take their turn as the provider of the feast and to present a paper on a subject of general interest. Member Norman Rockwell fulfilled both duties for many years in that room upstairs. Today you can still dine there, although no one stands to call order and give a speech. The restaurant is the Brew Works.

The revitalization continues and the octogenarian who enjoyed Saturdays in Pittsfield will live to see the movie theater where she and her mother watched Nelson Eddy reopen on North Street. The new economic prosperity will bring the renovation and reuse of the Stanley Works, evoking the boom of the first Gilded Age when the growth of Pittsfield started with the train, the courthouse, Government Mill and the Stanley Works. Still, there is more to do.

A quarter century ago Berkshire cottages all over the county were standing in disrepair, boarded and silent. Slowly, in South County, they were purchased, restored and reused. Blantyre, Cranwell, Elm Court, The Mount, Ventfort Hall, Wheatleigh and more were revitalized and formed the underpinning of the tourist economy in South County. In Pittsfield, Tor Court was transformed into a hospital, and some former cottages remain private homes. But...

Preservation Massachusetts placed the William Russell Allen House on its "Ten Most Endangered List." The historic structures most worth saving based upon architectural importance, the importance of the people who lived there and the events that took place there are on that list. When placed on the National Register for Historic Places, the William Russell Allen House was cited as "the finest example of the Queen Anne style extant in Pittsfield and one of the finest in Berkshire County." Saving the house saves the story of a family, and a city. Yet it stands neglected, boarded shut and crumbling.

In the great revitalization of the twenty-first century, the more that is saved, the more of the city's story, character and beauty can be preserved. The story of Pittsfield is made whole again from its unpretentious beginnings through the muscular and ingenious Gilded Age. If the present day is not a second Gilded Age in Pittsfield, then it is at least a gilt-edged age, shining and full of promise. Fifty or a hundred years hence, historians will applaud these efforts in Pittsfield, save evidence of these triumphs and tell an unbroken story of more than three hundred years of Pittsfield's survival and growth.

NOTES

INTRODUCING THE GILDED AGE

1. Mark Twain, and Charles Dudley Warner, *The Gilded Age: A Tale of To-day* (Chicago, IL: F.G. Gilman, 1873).
2. From William Dean Howells, "Society," in *Stops of Various Quills* (New York: Harper Brothers, 1895).
3. Quoted from notes in notebooks discovered by biographer R.W.B. Lewis, which can be found at Bieneke Library, Yale University.
4. Henry James sent copies of his books to family members and on the fly leaf or in an accompanying letter, he commented on his work. This is a comment made to a cousin in Stockbridge, Massachusetts, accompanying a book, and unfortunately the Stockbridge house, Strawberry Hill, burned to the ground, destroying the James first editions and notations. This quote was repeated to the author from memory.
5. See Matthew Josephson, *The Robber Barons: The Great American Capitalists 1861–1901* (New York: Harcourt, Brace and Co., 1934).
6. See Russell Lynes, *The Tastemakers* (New York: Harper, 1954).
7. Eleanor Dwight, *The Gilded Age: Edith Wharton and Her Contemporaries* (New York: Universe Pub., 1996).
8. See Ron Chernow, *The Life of John D. Rockefeller, Sr.* (New York, NY: Random House, 1999) and *The House of Morgan* (New York: Simon & Schuster, 1990).
9. Cleveland Amory, *The Last Resorts* (New York, NY: Harper, 1952).

THE COTTAGERS OF PITTSFIELD

10. Brooke Astor, in conversation with the author.
11. Acceptance letter from Thomas Allen to the people of Pittsfield, reprinted in *New England*.
12. All Allen quotes are from a twenty-two page document in the Allen family private papers. The document is unsigned and undated.
13. *The Berkshire Hills*, December 1902, collection of the Berkshire Athenaeum.
14. Ecclesiastes 10:19.
15. See *Artistic Country-Seats; Types of Recent American Villa & Cottage Architecture with Instances of Country Club-Houses* (New York: Appleton, 1886–7).
16. Quote reported years later in the *Berkshire Eagle* when they were debating whether to call them concerts "under the stairs" or "under the moon."

AMERICA'S GILT COMPLEX

17. The Fauntleroy suit created a major fad for formal dress for American middle-class children. Burnett wrote in *Little Lord Fauntleroy*: "What the Earl saw was a graceful, childish figure in a black velvet suit, with a lace collar, and with lovelocks waving about the handsome, manly little face, whose eyes met his with a look of innocent good-fellowship." *Wikipedia Online Encyclopedia*, s.v. "Little Lord Fauntleroy," http://en.wikipedia.org/wiki/Little_Lord_Fauntleroy.

GILDED AGE PHILANTHROPY

18. See Andrew Carnegie, *The Gospel of Wealth and Other Timely Essays* (New York: Century, 1900).

INTRODUCING PITTSFIELD

19. See Edward Boltwood, *The History of Pittsfield, Massachusetts, From the Year 1876 to the Year 1916* (Pittsfield, MA: The City of Pittsfield, 1916).
20. Minutes of the Pittsfield Town Meeting, April 1872.

MONEY AND POWER: PITTSFIELD IN THE GILDED AGE

21. *Etiquette of Letter Writing* (Pittsfield, MA: Eaton, Crane & Pike, 1906).
22. W.M. Crane, telegram to Crane & Company, Dalton, July 21, 1886, Crane Museum archives.

THEY GOT IT ALL IN PITTSFIELD

23. *Pittsfield Evening Eagle*, December 16, 1872.

ABOUT THE AUTHOR

Author and lecturer Dr. Carole Owens has been named Scholar in Residence by the Massachusetts Foundation for the Humanities and Museum Scholar at the Berkshire Historical Society. She has written eight books, including *The Berkshire Cottages* (1984) and *The Lost Days of Agatha Christie* (1996), and she has been a contributor to a number of periodicals, such as the *Boston Globe* and *Ladies Home Journal*, and a columnist for the *Berkshire Eagle*. She has been a talking head and consultant for television programs on A&E, PBS, the Travel Channel, the History Channel, Fox News and cable access and local news. In addition, she has lectured at the Cooper-Hewitt National Design Museum, the National Trust for Historic Preservation and the Smithsonian, as well as over six hundred talks at historical societies, universities and libraries.